ANNE HALL DICK LLB, NP

Anne Hall Dick is a solicitor with a special interest in family law and mediation. She is a partner in a private practice with offices in Glasgow and Kilmarnock, and is also a part-time Tribunal Chairman and a mediator.

These areas of work—together with her involvement at various times in her local Citizen's Advice Bureau and Woman's Aid Association, the Strathclyde Family Conciliation Service, the Scottish Child Law Centre, and as founder chairman of the Family Law Association and founder convener of CALM (Comprehensive Accredited Lawyer Mediators), as well as her experience in providing mediation training in Scotland and England—have made her increasingly aware of how important it is for people to have access to information about the law when they are facing family breakdown.

This book is the result.

D1146407

BREAKING UP

WITHOUT FALLING APART

ANNE HALL DICK LLB, NP

Illustrations by ALEX LEONARD

B&W PUBLISHING · EDINBURGH

First published 1993
This edition published 1996 by
B&W Publishing Ltd., Edinburgh
ISBN 1 873631 62 6
© Anne Hall Dick 1996
Illustrations © Alex Leonard 1996

British Library Cataloguing in Publication Data:
A catalogue record for this book is available
from the British Library.

CONTENTS

ACKNOWLEDGEMENTS

Grateful thanks to all the people who good-naturedly toiled towards the creation of the first edition of this book: to Karen Barr who translated my scribbled hieroglyphics into a first draft; and Vivienne Ross, then a student at Dundee University, now a trainee solicitor, for assisting with practical research; to Jessica Burns of the Independent Tribunal Service; Michael Clancy of The Law Society of Scotland; Eve Crowe of the Scottish Legal Aid Board; Hugh Donald of Shepherd & Wedderburn WS; Caroline Graham of Macleod & MacCallum, Solicitors; R MacKenzie of Moores Rowland, Chartered Accountants; Walter Nicol of Strathclyde Family Mediation Service; Anne Provan, sessional counsellor with Anne Hall Dick & Co., Solicitors; to others who read over that draft, made most useful and welcome suggestions, gently reunited some of my split infinitives and corrected the more creative spelling; and to Peter Hayman for his design flair.

Since there has been much moving of the goalposts in the area of family law since that edition, further thanks are now due to many of those original stalwarts, and also to Moira Jeffrey, trainee solicitor with Anne Hall Dick and Co., Susie McLeod of Shepherd and Wedderburn WS, and to Debbie Gray and Sandra Park for their administrative labours.

I claim all credit for any lurking errors or imperfections.

INTRODUCTION

This book has some pages which will seem more important to you than others.

Look at the list of Contents.

Read through the sections which deal with the questions you have been asking. Then perhaps at some time have a look at the other pages, because they will help you to understand the whole picture.

Going through a separation is never easy.

It is best to cope with it a bit at a time. If you have the right attitude and the right help, you will probably find that one day you will look back and see that what you have been through has made you grow stronger. However, even if you do have the right attitude and the right help, there will still be times when you feel you cannot cope.

Be patient with yourself and **don't panic!**

Make full use of this book. Think of it as a notebook— there are pages where you can fill in information that would be useful to keep. There are sheets at the back for you to jot down notes, reminders, appointments—or satisfying swear words if that would make you feel better! Put a big rubber band round it, so you can keep together the letters and other papers you are likely to accumulate.

Quite a lot of the information is likely to change because there are so many developments in Family Law, and in the organisations dealing with family breakdown. The information is as up to date as possible at the end of January 1996.

So good luck!

Remember that the word 'crisis' in Chinese is said to be made up from the pictograms for 'danger' and 'opportunity'. Hopefully this book will help you minimise the dangers and maximise the opportunities.

1

YOU'RE THINKING ABOUT SEPARATING

Separation solves some problems and causes others—all you can do is deal with the difficulties as and when they arise. It is important, though, to allow yourself plenty of time, and to be ready to seek help when necessary.

Because separation causes so much upset and hurt, the first thing to do is to consider very honestly and carefully whether there is any chance of saving the relationship. Marriage counselling or individual counselling can be invaluable here, and, even if separation still occurs, counselling is likely to make the process easier all round.

Remember that if you have children they will usually want you very much to stay together. This is not necessarily the best thing for them, but you must be sure enough of what you are doing to be able to cope with the children's reaction.

Be very practical—think of the mundane day-to-day things that would have to be sorted out. Remember that the money coming in to the house when you're together in one household will not go so far between two households.

For names and addresses of counselling agencies
☞ Chapter 26

For discussion on finance
☞ Chapters 18-20

For details of organisations which can offer help and support

☞ p113-5

If your partner has a drink problem or is violent to you and will not go for help, or perhaps will not even acknowledge the fact, then it might be more urgent for you to get out of the relationship. It might also be helpful for you to have specialised support.

One thing you have to accept is that if you don't like your partner's behaviour, and your partner doesn't think there's anything wrong with it, then you can't make your partner change. You must either find some way of living with the situation, or leave the relationship. Living with a partner who for some reason is behaving badly to you can have a terrible effect on your self-confidence.

Try to make your decision while you still have enough energy to use for the future!

If you do decide to separate, you must not expect your partner or your children to accept your decision without some hurt or anger. However, don't spend too much time in trying to justify your decision to other people—even your partner. Doing this usually involves underlining or exaggerating the faults of your partner, and only causes more bitterness.

If you have children, make it a priority to arrange matters so that the children suffer as little confusion and uncertainty as possible. For example, if you have become involved with someone else, be careful how you explain this to the children and make the introductions. If your partner has become involved with someone else, be just as careful.

Don't rush it!

Bear in mind that decisions tend not to be black or white—it's a matter of finding the shade of grey that fits best.

If you decide to separate, and you are the main source of income, don't offer more financial support than you can realistically manage. Sometimes people do this because they feel bad about hurting their partner, and they think such an offer will soften the blow.

Well—it might at that point. Then it will become obvious to you that the amount you're left with won't keep you alive, or won't allow you a roof over your head. If you have to backtrack on the offer it will feel worse for your partner than if you'd never made it.

Equally, don't leap to the opposite extreme.

Be realistic.

If, on the other hand, you are not the main earner, don't be so eager to get out of the relationship that you insist on giving up any possible claims you might have. Money claims on separation are generally about fair sharing and practicalities—not blame apportionment or assuaging feelings of guilt.

It is important to disentangle the emotional side of separating from the money side.

TO THINK ABOUT

If you've made the decision to separate, the priorities are:

The children: think about a referral to the Mediation Service.

Practicalities: a consultation with a sympathetic lawyer can help stop things going into a downward spiral.

Choosing and using a solicitor

☞ Chapters 4 & 5

2

YOUR PARTNER HAS MADE THE DECISION TO SEPARATE

This is a 100% 'rug being pulled out from under your feet' situation. It is frighteningly cold and lonely for most people.

If your partner had died, you would at least have happy memories to look back on. As it is, you probably feel that the pain of what is happening now spoils the past as well. Even taking one day at a time at this stage may seem like a tall order. It is important to keep in mind that if you can just put one foot in front of the other and plod through the practical things that come up, then at some point the weight will start lifting.

You will probably feel very drained. Try to use the energy you have to deal with the present, rather than constantly thinking over what went wrong. Begin to paint a picture of what could be salvaged from the wreckage to build the best that can be achieved for the future.

You may feel almost overwhelmed by quite violent emotions from time to time. This does happen. It will get less if you just *accept* that you're feeling that way now but you won't always.

Don't fight it but don't feed it.

Talking to friends and relatives can help, but remember that although they will want you to feel better they will be feeling upset too. It can therefore be a good idea to talk things over with someone who is not involved, such as a counsellor.

For names and addresses of counselling organisations
☞p108-110

If you have children then they will probably be upset too. It is very important to see that, although you are all hurt, you are not all in the same position. The relationship you had with your partner is ending. The relationship the children have with their other parent goes on. It is considered very important for the children to keep contact with both parents, except in very unusual circumstances.

If the children are living with you, then once the dust has settled you should find it helpful to have the other parent still making a practical contribution. Try not to have a gap in contact.

You may find that it is just too upsetting to be present at the handover. If so, try to arrange for a friend or relative to be there instead until you can cope with seeing your partner. A referral to the Family Mediation Service could be very helpful.

Addresses
☞ p111

If your partner is involved with someone else then you might feel strongly that the children shouldn't see that other person. For a little while after the separation it might indeed be better for the children not to have to deal with a new person—they will have a massive change to cope with anyway. However, there will come a point quite soon when it will almost certainly be important for them to meet.

For a detailed discussion concerning children and conciliation (mediation)
☞ Chapter 7

Remember, they're not being introduced to a replacement parent. They'll be meeting someone who is a friend of their mum or dad. For the children to remain close to the other parent, and in order to prevent the situation becoming artificial, then they need to meet. This will not be easy for you to cope with, but if you can it will be a huge help to the children.

If the children are based with your partner, then when you see them try not to rub in how unhappy you are. They will probably be very anxious about you anyway.

While on the subject of minimising anxiety, try to keep very closely to arrangements you make about contact with the children. If you're quarter of an hour late picking the children up, then they and their other parent will be getting more and more worried about whether you're going to turn up. When you do arrive

'It began to dawn on Felicity that she and Giles really had very little in common.'

the atmosphere will be tense—and an argument all too likely. Similarly, if you're quarter of an hour late bringing them back, your partner will probably be imagining that you're on your way to Australia, and will again be so tense that when you do turn up sparks will fly.

Finally, a reminder to be realistic where money is concerned. If you are the main earner, avoid making financial arrangements that are really bribes. If you offer a lot more than you can reasonably afford, in order to try to make your partner see you in a better light, you're likely to remain separated and very poor!

See also the comments on making financial arrangements in Chapter 1

☞ p3

TO THINK ABOUT

If your partner has decided to leave, your priorities are:

The children: separate out your interests from those of the children—a referral to the Mediation Service can help.

Practicalities: taking advice from a sympathetic lawyer can help to make some of the practical problems more manageable.

For information about choosing and using a solicitor

☞ Chapters 4 & 5

3

YOU HAVE AGREED TO SEPARATE

If the relationship is definitely over and you can separate amicably, that's great!

Any children involved will be much better able to cope than if there are lots of arguments. You'll be able to keep the happy memories you have without feeling they're spoiled.

For a detailed discussion on children and mediation

☞ Chapter 7

Even if there are no obvious problems concerning the children, it might be helpful, perhaps before you tell the children, to use the Family Mediation Service. A mediator can help you to make sure you've thought things through from the children's point of view.

Preliminary advice from a solicitor might be wise— it can help in avoiding unexpected pitfalls.

Sometimes people want to have a friendly separation, but find that their ideas of what constitutes a fair financial split are much further apart than they would have expected.

For details of the rules regarding the financial split on divorce

☞ Chapters 18 & 19

Sometimes people make informal agreements between themselves, only to discover when they take legal advice that they have more rights than they realised.

Take legal advice before you shake hands on something.

Anything other than the most simple agreement usually has to be drawn up in a fairly technical way if it is to be relied on in the future.

For a discussion on Separation Agreements

☞ Chapter 8

Another complicating factor can be the appearance of a new partner on the scene. Even if the new relationship only starts after the separation, it can make the other person feel more hurt and threatened than they might have expected. Things should settle down again eventually, but don't feel too dismayed if there are some hiccups.

Any separation—even if agreed by both partners—brings about big changes, which uncover unexpected insecurities and anxieties. Just accept that there are likely to be bumpy patches, and fasten your seat belt ready for when you hit them!

4

CHOOSING A SOLICITOR

For many people, this is the first time they've had to see a lawyer. (The kind of lawyer you talk to will almost certainly be a solicitor, rather than the other type of lawyer, an advocate.) For most of the rest, any other contact will have been to do with buying a house or making a Will.

It may feel very daunting to think of having to discuss very private and emotional matters with a solicitor. In fact, it should help.

There are a number of ways of choosing a solicitor. Personal recommendation is a good one—if someone you know has had a solicitor for the same sort of thing and you like the sound of their approach, then you should phone the office and make an appointment, giving the name of the solicitor involved. Most firms have more than one solicitor, and often each one tends to practise in different areas of law.

You can ask for a list of lawyers in your area who have a particular interest in family law. Another way is to contact the Law Society of Scotland or the Family Law Association.

Addresses
☞ p113-4

You could phone your local Citizens' Advice Bureau and explain that you have separated or are about to separate and are looking for a lawyer. They can give the details of local firms dealing in this type of work.

If you prefer to use *Yellow Pages* or a similar directory, you may find that legal firms sometimes have advertisements showing their particular specialities. Look for the terms '**matrimonial**', '**consistorial**', or '**family law**'. If there is no indication in the entry as to whether the firm you choose does family law, then when you phone for an appointment explain very generally what it's about.

If you might need Legal Aid, then check when you phone up whether the firm deals with Legal Aid cases. Some firms, particularly in the cities, don't.

For details of Legal Aid

☞ Chapter 24

"How much is that one . . . ?"

11

5

USING A SOLICITOR

Most solicitors have a system of appointments—don't expect to be able to see one immediately. You might be lucky and find that someone can see you at once, but usually you'll have to wait for a few days, and sometimes a little longer.

If you know you're not going to be able to keep an appointment, do let the office know—it might let someone else have an earlier appointment.

At quite an early stage—possibly the first meeting—your solicitor will need some basic details. Sometimes it's difficult to remember things when you're a little nervous, so it could help if you note down the required information beforehand. There are forms at the end of this book which set out the type of information your solicitor is likely to ask for.

Forms for noting down relevant information

☞ Chapter 27

Take your **children's birth certificates** and your **marriage certificate** with you if you have them.

If you have been married before and divorced take in the **divorce papers**.

If there are specific questions you want to ask, write them down—you could use the notes pages at the back of this book, if it will help to keep things together in one place—and leave space to jot down the answers.

You might want to take a friend or relative to the office for company, but it's usually better if you go in to see the lawyer on your own. Even if it's someone you like and trust very much, some of what they remember and what they think you should do will get mixed in, and this may confuse matters.

Another point is that the person you take with you could turn out to be a useful witness for you, if matters end up in court. It is therefore important that information about what has been going on is taken from you separately.

If you feel you won't be able to remember all that you're being told, you could ask your solicitor if your friend or relative could come in for five minutes at the end, in order to listen to a summary of main points. This will allow you to discuss the options better afterwards.

Don't ever be worried about telling your lawyer if you change your mind regarding what you want to do. Your lawyer will want to help you get the best out of the situation.

For instance, if you start some sort of legal action, and your partner then realises that his or her behaviour has simply not been acceptable, you may well wish to stop the court action and enjoy a successful reconciliation.

Whatever you do, you must keep in touch. No lawyer can do what is necessary unless you provide proper instructions.

If for any reason you feel unhappy about the advice you're being given, try to work out:

—Is it the legal rules that you don't like?— Sometimes the rules don't fit in with the way you feel, but the solicitor still has to tell you them. It is then a case of 'don't shoot the messenger'!

—Is it the way you're being told the information you don't like?—If so, try again. Ask questions if there is anything you don't understand, and tell your solicitor if you're puzzled or if the reply is unclear.

Sometimes clients appear much more composed than they feel. They seem to be taking in information when they're not! Don't worry about saying you don't understand—it's the solicitor's job to explain the legal rules in a way that makes sense. Just remember that solicitors need some feedback—so that they know how they're doing!

If Things Go Wrong

If you and your solicitor are not communicating well, it's usually better to try to get on a better footing than to change solicitors, since such a change will only add to the complexity of the situation. The first solicitor will probably want their bill paid before they hand over your papers—a solicitor has the right to keep your papers until you've paid the bill.

If you're receiving Legal Aid, it can take a while to have all the paperwork completed to transfer the Legal Aid to the new solicitor, and delays might not be to your advantage. There are some circumstances, particularly if it's not the first move, in which the transfer might not be allowed.

It is also more difficult from the new solicitor's point of view to pick things up in the middle.

It may happen that the relationship between you and your solicitor breaks down completely and can't be mended. If this happens then of course you should change solicitors. If things have really gone wrong you might consider making a complaint to the Law Society of Scotland, if you believe your solicitor is at fault.

Address

☞ p114

The Law Society has a legal duty to look into complaints of professional misconduct and inadequate professional services. You can find out more about their powers from the leaflet *Complaints Against Solicitors*, which is available from the Society.

TO THINK ABOUT

A solicitor is there to advise you, to give you information and to help you think through the possible choices. A solicitor is *not* there to tell you what to do. You are the one who is going to have to live with the consequences!

It is important that you have a good relationship with your solicitor, that you feel you are being told things in a way you understand, and that you're being kept informed. The best way is to be careful choosing in the first place!

15

6

PAYING FOR A SOLICITOR

You'll probably want to know how much a solicitor's services will cost. Unfortunately, it's very difficult to predict this because it's so uncertain how much work will be involved.

A great deal depends on you and your partner. If the negotiations or court action go on and on with frequent meetings, telephone calls and letters, the legal fees will increase.

If you are receiving Benefit, or are on a low income, you may qualify for Legal Aid. If you don't qualify for Legal Aid, the final cost is likely to be worked out by adding up the cost of each meeting, telephone call, letter and document. The Law Society of Scotland provide a recommended table of fees for solicitors. These fees take into account information concerning how much solicitors have to pay out for staff, professional indemnity insurance and fees, premises and so on.

As an example, the hourly rate they recommended from 1st January 1996 was £86, though the rate usually changes each year. Bear in mind that this rate is only a guideline—some solicitors charge more than the recommended amount, and some less. At the outset,

Legal Aid

☞ Chapter 24

you should ask your chosen firm for details of their hourly rate.

You will also be asked to pay what are known as **outlays**—the costs of, for example, specialist reports, valuations, or surveys. Remember, too, that VAT is chargeable on your solicitor's fee.

To gain some idea of the scale of legal fees, consider the following. If you want to divorce your partner because of their unreasonable behaviour or adultery, and if the action is not opposed, the legal expenses you could ask your partner to pay back to you would be the legal fee of roughly between £460 and £620 plus VAT plus outlays (at 1995/1996 figures). The outlays are quite high—they include a court fee of £70 to start the action, and another £32 which has to be paid to the court before the action is finalised. These costs are likely to go up.

Grounds for divorce

☞ Chapter 16

If the divorce includes anything else, such as Orders concerning children, an extra amount of around £200 has to be added, plus VAT. There might be extra expenses for work not included in the basic action, which could not be claimed back.

It's unlikely that you would get the costs back if the divorce was based on two years' separation. You and your partner could agree to share the costs of course, though you would still be responsible for paying your own lawyer in the first place.

As you can see, costs are often liable to escalate. For this reason, they should always be discussed at the outset, so that you know where you stand.

If you can use the **simplified divorce procedure** then the cost is very much less. In fact you don't need to use a lawyer, although you might prefer to let your solicitor sort out the paperwork if you're allergic to forms.

Simplified Divorce Procedure

☞ p57

If you're involved in an **opposed** (**defended**) court action, the legal costs depend on the number of court appearances, as well as the amount of paperwork and the frequency of meetings, letters and telephone calls. In addition there are other expenses, such as the shorthand writer who notes the evidence, and witnesses—including perhaps a child psychologist, actuary or surveyor.

It all adds up! An agreed settlement, worked out quite early on, can be a *very* sensible idea, unless there is too large a gap between what seems reasonable to you and what seems reasonable to your partner.

One final point regarding who pays court costs: if you have got all or most of what you wanted in court, you might feel that your partner should be made to stump up for your costs. Traditionally the person who 'won' was usually able also to recover their costs from the other person. Nowadays actions between couples tend to be very complicated, with requests on both sides, and often the outcome is a partial success for both.

Quite often the court says that each person should be responsible for their own costs. This is not always the case, but the possibility has to be kept in mind!

Furthermore, if you don't have Legal Aid and your partner does, then it's even more likely that you will end up paying at least your own costs, even if the outcome seems favourable to you.

7

MEDIATION (CONCILIATION)

'Conciliation' is a rather confusing word. Sometimes people think it means the same as 'reconciliation'. In fact, it is the same as **'mediation'**.

The process of mediation involves a separating couple sitting down together in a neutral place with a trained mediator who will help them make decisions about their future.

The mediator doesn't make the decisions. His or her aim is to help the couple to identify the issues to be discussed, focus on the common ground, explore possible options and work towards a solution which will be acceptable to all concerned.

Where this process works it achieves something which is almost impossible to achieve by any other method of resolving disputes—it helps the people involved to understand one another better. It also helps them understand better how any children involved are likely to be feeling.

You might feel very nervous about sitting down with your partner, even if someone else is there. For some people it is one of the most difficult things to do. This is quite natural, but it's usually better just to grasp the nettle and do it! The mediator will realise how tough it has been to agree to come, and will help you to cope.

Furthermore, confronting the anxiety you feel should help to liberate you from some of the paralysing hurt.

The first meeting usually takes at least an hour, often a little longer. Generally, more than one meeting is necessary. An important starting point in mediation is that the best solution to the problems you face is one which is genuinely agreed between you and your partner. It is important that your discussions are frank, and therefore you should both accept that they are confidential, until such time as you both want to have something binding put in writing. Legal rules are about to be introduced to ensure that what is discussed in mediation is not referred to later unless you both want this. These rules will apply in most circumstances.

Remember—since the children will almost certainly love you both, it will help them greatly if both parents are able to talk face to face without arguing. Indeed, if there is a court action under way to deal with issues relating to your children, one option for the court is to tell you to try mediation.

If you both want to go to mediation then it's never too early or too late! Mediation can take place either before or after a separation. It's usually helpful to go to mediation early on, but in some cases mediation has taken place years after separation.

Just keep in mind that the meeting is on neutral ground.

There are local services all over Scotland with trained mediators for dealing with child related issues. **Family Mediation Scotland** is the umbrella organisation. Some of these services are beginning to offer mediation on financial matters as well as child related issues.

For a list of addresses

☞ p111

The Law Society of Scotland has a procedure to

enable experienced family lawyers with training in mediation skills to offer mediation in both child and property matters. If you are interested in that possibility contact the Law Society and ask for information about **accredited family mediators**.

Address
☞ p114

Most family law mediators are members of **CALM** (Comprehensive Accredited Lawyer Mediators). The secretary of CALM can give you a list of members in your area.

Address
☞ p112

When lawyers work as mediators they provide information about the legal framework. They help you to assemble the information you need concerning the financial side, and to think through the various possible

"Here, wait a minute—the on/off switch is on your side!"

options, and their consequences, in making plans for your children as well as yourselves. Remember, though, that a lawyer mediator can be used even if there are no children involved.

The cost of the mediation is generally shared between you. If you are getting help under the Legal Aid scheme then your share of the cost could be met by Legal Aid, although if you obtain a settlement in the end the cost of the mediation might be recovered from that. It's important to remember, though, that your advising solicitor (not the lawyer mediator) would have to ask the Legal Aid Board for permission before mediation starts.

A summary of the proposals you have made would be sent to each of you, and then to your advising solicitor when you want your decision to be made legally binding. A summary of the financial information can also be drawn up by the mediator.

Separation
Agreements

☞ Chapter
8

Mediation can lead to a **Separation Agreement**, or to the terms you agree being included in a **Court Order** if there is a court action under way.

TO THINK ABOUT

It seems that much of the damage children suffer after a separation comes not so much from the separation itself, but from the way it is handled.

It is the responsibility of both parents, and it is also in their interest, to shield their children from the adult problems.

8

SEPARATION AGREEMENTS

If you both accept that your relationship is over, it's a good idea to arrange the practical matters by negotiation.

The basis of an Agreement could be reached using mediation. You would then each have your own advising solicitors check over the terms, which could then be put into a binding Agreement.

☞ Previous Chapter

Alternatively, you could each discuss the various options with your own solicitors, and work out realistic possibilities. The two solicitors would then write to one another with proposals and counter proposals, hopefully working towards a solution that will be acceptable to all concerned.

This would usually take into account the rules concerning money upon divorce, even if, as is often the case, there are no plans to divorce until after a two-year separation.

Financial division of matrimonial property is dealt with in Chapters 18 & 19.

In some circumstances it can be helpful for you and your partner and the two solicitors all to get together for a discussion.

Once everything is agreed, it can be set out in a document called a **Separation Agreement** (sometimes known as a **Minute of Agreement**). This can be worded in such a way as to have the same force as a Court Order so far as the financial side is concerned.

Areas Covered by an Agreement

The Agreement can cover as much or as little as you want. You could simply agree about financial support for a trial period of separation. However, if you are going to the effort of having a written document prepared, you're more likely to want it to cover all of the outstanding matters—so that if you do get divorced you will only need a minimum of help from the courts.

A Separation Agreement usually deals with where the children are going to live, and what contact there should be with the other parent. Decisions relating to children set out in a Separation Agreement do not have the same force as a Court Order, but in most cases provide a reliable enough framework. If there was any real danger of children being whisked out of Britain by the other parent, a Court Order would be safer—but if matters were as adversarial as that, it's unlikely that you would be considering a Separation Agreement!

Court Orders relating to Children

☞ Chapter 12

Depending on how the division of the joint matrimonial property is decided, the Agreement may be able to allow for the family home to be sold and, if so, to define what share you and your partner should each receive. Alternatively, the house and loan might be transferred from joint names to one person. If the house is rented, the tenancy could change hands. The question of occupancy rights might also have to be dealt with.

Division of the contents can be sorted out, preferably with a common-sense approach, to reflect the practical needs of all concerned.

24

Quite often there might be a joint endowment policy. It should be decided whether this is to be maintained, transferred to one person, surrendered or sold. It is not usually a good idea to surrender a policy, but sometimes it's a practical option.

For a discussion on division of the matrimonial home

☞ Chapters 18 & 19

You would want to sort out what's to happen to any car or cars you own, allowing for any loan still being repaid.

If dealing with the house doesn't leave both of you with a fair share of the matrimonial property, there may be a **capital payment** to be made. The Agreement should detail not just the amount, but how and when it has to be paid, and whether any interest should be added on until payment is complete.

You might well both agree to give up any claim you could have had against the estate of the other person on death. Just because a married couple separate doesn't mean that their succession rights end automatically. It's nearly always a good idea to draw up a Will at the same time as a Separation Agreement.

The question of ongoing financial support should also be dealt with. Money payable for a wife (or husband if appropriate) will usually have a cut-off date. **Aliment** for children is likely to be affected by the **Child Support Agency**.

Financial support for children

☞ Chapter 20

Even if you both agree an amount for child support, the Child Support Agency will fix their own figure according to their formula if the parent looking after the children receives Income Support, Family Credit or Disability Working Allowance. Furthermore, if the formula produces a higher figure than the one agreed, the parent with the children can ask the Child Support Agency to deal with the child support side despite the Agreement, although not necessarily straight away because of the phasing-in provisions of the Agency.

Explanation of the role of the Child Support Agency

☞ Chapter 23

In addition to the Child Support Agency's right to overrule an agreed figure, there will generally be a provision allowing any financial support set out in the Agreement to be reviewed if there is a change in circumstances.

The Agreement will be rounded off with your consent to have it **registered for preservation and execution**. Although this sounds alarmingly like sanctioning capital punishment, it allows for the possibility of chopping off money rather than heads! It allows the registered Agreement to be enforced in the ways that a Court Order can, for example enabling the deduction of money from the wages of an employed person.

The Agreement can include any other terms that are appropriate and that you both accept.

There may be other documents to be prepared in order for some of the agreed steps to be carried out. For instance, if a house transfer is involved then a document known as a **Disposition** has to be signed to change the ownership, and a **Deed** is needed to sort out responsibility for the secured loan.

Since an Agreement can be challenged in the future if it wasn't fair at the time it was drawn up, it is important that you both consider all the legal options, and that the terms are not totally lopsided!

9

INCOME TAX

If you and your partner are married and separate, and if you believe it is going to be permanent, you should tell your tax office. Your employer can tell you which one to contact. If you're self-employed and have an accountant you should tell your accountant.

To make it easier to describe the rules, the word **'spouse'** will be used to mean either husband or wife. 'Partner' isn't accurate because many of these rules only apply to married couples.

Remember that the tax year runs from 6th April in one year to 5th April the following year.

Tax Allowances

Everyone can earn a certain amount without paying tax, by claiming what is called a **personal allowance**. Many people who are married or have children can claim an additional allowance even if the couple separate.

The rules changed considerably in 1988, and if there is any chance the old rules might apply then ask your tax office for leaflet IR93.

The Tax Year You Separate

In the tax year you separate you continue to receive the **married couples' allowance** for that tax year. From 1993/94 this has been a joint allowance. It is given to the husband first unless the wife chooses to have half given to her.

If you're the mother and are looking after the children you can claim the **additional personal allowance** for that year. If you already have half of a married couples' allowance, as mentioned in the last paragraph, then the amount of the additional personal allowance may be restricted to reflect this.

Subsequent Tax Years

If you're bringing up the children you can claim the additional personal allowance. If you and your partner

"Right—which half of the overdraft do you want?"

are each bringing up one or more of the children this allowance can be shared. For the allowance to be applicable, the children must be under 16 or in further education.

If you're not bringing up the children but you are paying money to their parent, then you'll be able to get some tax relief on those payments if:

—You are making the payments under the terms of a Court Order, binding Separation Agreement, or Child Support Agency Assessment , **and**

Court Orders

☞ Chapter 12

—The payments are to your divorced or separated spouse, **and**

Separation Agreements

☞ Chapter 8

—He or she has not remarried, **and**

CSA Assessments

☞ Chapter 23

—The payments are for the maintenance of your spouse or a child under 21 of yours or accepted as a child of your family.

If you do manage to get over all these hurdles the maximum amount of tax relief you can get will be a limit equal to the married couples' allowance.

Just bear in mind that if your spouse remarries you'll lose the tax relief. You should tell the tax office if this happens. On the other hand, if you remarry you continue getting tax relief.

If you're receiving **maintenance payments** you will not have to pay tax on them. Your spouse has to pay the full amount to you then sort out any tax relief with their tax office.

10

THE FAMILY HOME

You might be worried in case your partner tells you to leave the family home or wants to sell it, or you might want to make them leave.

Married Couples

If you're married then it doesn't matter whether you or your partner is the owner or tenant of the house you share, known as the **matrimonial home**. You both have **occupancy rights**—the legal right to live there.

The non-owner or non-tenant will usually lose their occupancy rights when a divorce is granted, or at an earlier stage if a court grants an Order to suspend their occupancy rights and exclude them from the house—known as an **Exclusion Order**.

Even on divorce it is still possible for you to ask the court to grant you sole occupancy rights for a specific period after the divorce. Often people prefer to have the question of the family home cut and dried by the time a divorce is granted. In fact, most people like to have the house either transferred or sold by then.

While you're married, it is difficult for an owned matrimonial home to be sold, unless you both consent. Whether it belongs to one or both of you, you both have to sign some of the paperwork before the sale can be finalised.

The courts can be asked to allow a sale to go ahead, although an action like this is unlikely to be successful if the one who opposes the sale is still living there and has nowhere else suitable to go. Nowadays the most common reason for the sale of a matrimonial home against the wishes of one (or sometimes both) of the couple is repossession actions by Building Societies or Banks for non-payment of the secured loan.

To persuade the court to give you an Exclusion Order you have to prove to the Sheriff that your partner's behaviour is putting you or your children's mental or physical health at risk. The proof will usually be given to the court in written statements known as **affidavits**, which are signed on oath in front of a Notary Public (usually your solicitor).

For information on requesting Interim Exclusion Orders

 p61

You have to provide an affidavit and so does a witness. A medical report from your GP, detailing physical injuries or treatment for stress, can be used to support your case.

A **Power of Arrest** should be attached to the Exclusion Order. The Police are then told about the Order and Power of Arrest, and this gives them wider powers to sort things out if your partner does turn up.

An Exclusion Order can be requested whether the house is owned or rented. However, if there is a third party involved in owning or renting the house, or if it is used for a trade or profession, then an Exclusion Order might not be appropriate.

On divorce, it is possible to ask the court to transfer the tenancy or title of the matrimonial home, or to make an Order for it to be sold. It's even possible to ask for a court official to be given the authority to sign the necessary documents, if you think your partner won't co-operate over that. Even before a divorce it is possible to ask the court to transfer the tenancy of a rented house.

Where you ask for ownership of a house to be transferred to you alone, you have to show that this is fair, having regard to the split of the matrimonial property. You will usually also have to be able to take over responsibility for the secured loan, with the lender's consent.

Unmarried Couples

The position is very different for unmarried couples. If you're living with someone but not married to them, and your partner is the owner or tenant, then you have *no automatic occupancy rights*.

If you have been living like a married couple, and particularly if you have children, then you can ask the court to grant you occupancy rights. These are not granted automatically or indefinitely, but only for a few months. You can ask for them to be renewed for further short periods.

If an **Occupancy Order** is granted, then while it is in force a whole range of other possibilities open up— you can ask for an Exclusion Order with a Power of Arrest and, if it is rented property, for the tenancy to be transferred to your name.

When trying to decide what to do, bear in mind how helpful it would be for the children to stay in the family home. It won't always be a realistic option but they'll be coping with big changes as it is. Trying to make new friends or fit into a new school would be an extra stress which should be avoided if possible.

IN SUMMARY

When you're considering where you stand with regard to the family home, you should remember:

—There are no automatic rights if you're not married and not the owner or tenant, though you can ask the court for them.

—If you are married, then even if you are the owner or tenant your partner still has occupancy rights in the family home, even if they've moved out. If they change their mind they are likely to be able to move back in again!

—If you're married and living in the matrimonial home but your partner is the tenant, it's very important to sort out the tenancy either before the divorce is granted or in the divorce itself— so, if your partner won't agree to transfer the tenancy, you can ask for the court to do this in the court action.

The thing to avoid is to find yourself divorced and living in a house rented or owned by your ex-partner.

11

CHILDREN

When a couple are married, even if they are separated, they have *equal* rights and responsibilities so far as their children are concerned, unless there is a Court Order in force or a supervision requirement from the Children's Panel.

In practice, when the children are living mainly with one parent, that parent tends to become the one who has the greater say in decisions which affect them.

Having said that, it is usually best for children if both their parents maintain an active role after separation. In view of this, the legal rules are being changed to encourage this approach.

☞ Next Chapter

If a couple are not married then the father has *no automatic legal rights* even if his name is on the birth certificate. He has to ask the court to grant him rights if things can't be resolved by agreement.

However, once the new rules apply, probably in November 1996, then unmarried parents can agree in writing for the father to have the same rights as if they were married. The Agreement must be properly drawn up—rules are to be made detailing the form it must take. It has to be registered in Edinburgh, and once registered it can only be cancelled by a court.

When parents separate it is terribly important, and difficult, for them to remember that although they are no longer going to be a couple they will continue to be parents.

Children usually want their parents to stay together—they will be unhappy about the separation. Children should be able to love both parents without feeling guilty or disloyal. On the other hand they won't want to feel that one of their parents is a bad person.

More and more research is available on how children feel during a separation, and on how they turn out afterwards. It seems that children are often so frightened to rock the boat any more, and so anxious not to hurt their parents, that they hide their own feelings. In most cases the parents are quite unaware of how badly the children feel.

Although the separation itself is likely to upset the children, it is up to *both* parents to protect the children from the fallout. This is particularly difficult if you didn't want to separate in the first place.

You have to think about the long term, and hold on to the fact that your own relationship with the children later on is likely to be much better if you keep them out of the adult problems. The children are also likely to turn out happier and better adjusted. So will you probably!

Children are usually much more aware of what's going on than you'd realise. Uncertainty about the future can make them feel worse than the truth. They'll want to know where they're going to live and go to school and when they'll be with the other parent.

It is usually best to spare them the gory details of the reason for the separation. The main message for children from both parents should be that sometimes parents do separate, but they continue being parents and loving their children.

If you were the one who left the family home, it is quite likely that the children will feel hurt about that themselves. This is particularly true if you have a new partner, especially if that partner has children. Don't assume that, just because the children seem happy when they're with you, they are not upset. They might confide such feelings to the other parent.

Try to work with rather than against the other parent over this. Don't assume the children are being coached or indoctrinated. Similarly, don't leap to the telephone to protest if you are the main carer and the children return after access upset and full of complaints.

Children, like adults, take time to adjust after a separation. They have to work through various stages. This will show up in different ways, depending on

"It's your father who's got the keys, Avril—ask HIM why he won't drive us to the seaside."

their ages, from bed-wetting through tantrums to lack of concentration. The signs often peak after access but it is better that there should be visible signs of adjustment than silent suffering! **Make sure they realise that the separation isn't their fault.**

Both parents: beware of misreading your children's messages. A child will often say to each parent separately that they want to be with that parent. Both parents may interpret this as meaning: *'I want you to fight for me'*, and rush off into a bitter battle in court. Usually the child simply means *'I love you both. I don't want to choose, I just want you to stop fighting'*, and practical arrangements can generally be made which allow both parents to be truly involved in their children's lives.

TO THINK ABOUT

The message that comes across loud and clear is that the usual and normal thing for children to want is to continue to have a good relationship with both their parents without being exposed to bickering, arguing or being made to feel disloyal.

It's no fun being the meat in the sandwich!

12

COURT ORDERS RELATING TO CHILDREN

If the adults involved can't agree what has to happen, where the children are to stay, or who is to have contact with them, then the court has to be asked to make the decision.

Most cases are dealt with in the local courts known as **Sheriff Courts**, although some are dealt with in the **Court of Session** in Edinburgh.

It is not only biological (birth) parents who can ask for **Court Orders** concerning children—anyone who has an interest can apply, including step-parents, grandparents and other relatives.

The rights asked for could be quite narrow and specific, perhaps about isolated education or health issues.

Nearly all the Orders requested are about where the children are to be based and how much time they should spend with the other parent. Up until 1995 the labels to describe this were **custody** and **access**. However, it was felt that these terms made children sound like items of property to be fought over, with one parent the winner and the other the 'also ran'.

The Children (Scotland) Act was passed in 1995. It

will come into force in stages. Along with other major changes, this Act does away with the terms custody and access. It encourages continued joint parenting after separation—both parents are expected to be involved in making important decisions.

It must be stressed, though, that Court Orders should be regarded as a last resort—to be made only when agreement cannot be reached by discussion.

If Orders are made they'll be called **Residence Orders** if they relate to where children are to be based, or **Contact Orders** if they relate to the arrangements for keeping in touch with and spending time with the other parent. If the children are going to divide their time between parents then each parent could have a Residence Order specifying the arrangements.

If the court has to decide on very specific questions regarding something like school or health, it will be called a **Specific Issue Order**.

If the court is asked to stop a parent doing something because it would not be good for the child, this will be called an **Interdict**.

Remember, though, that the main idea is to avoid involving the courts at all!

Children's Views

The Act also says that parents must take their children's views into account when making a major decision which affects them. Children of 12 and over are assumed to be old enough to form a view; with younger children it would depend on how mature they were. Children can become involved directly in court actions affecting them, in order to give their views.

Nevertheless, don't just put your children in the driving seat and expect them to make all the decisions!

That won't help you or the children. Avoid making them feel that they're having to choose one parent and reject the other. Find out their hopes and fears, explain and discuss the possibilities, and try to make plans that will be as suitable for the children as possible.

As stated earlier, it is likely that this new framework will come into force in November 1996. The existing framework does refer to custody and access, so for completeness a brief description of these terms is given here.

Custody means the right to have the children living with you most of the time, and the right to take decisions about their education and health.

Access is the right to spend time with them—usually on a very clearly defined pattern.

If the court has to make a decision regarding custody, the **Sheriff** looks at the position from the point of view of what he or she thinks is best for the children.

Some mothers believe they have an automatic passport to custody—*not so*. There was a time when most dads worked and most mums stayed at home to look after the children. In those days the mum usually had the closer bond and for this and practical reasons usually got custody.

Nowadays, with rising unemployment but more working women, the pattern of child care is very different. It is true that the great majority of single parents are women, but a significant minority are men.

Equally, most parents assume that they have an absolute right to spend time with their children. Again—*not so*. If they have to ask a court for access they must show that their children will benefit from the contact.

The focus is supposed to be on parental responsibilities rather than rights.

It is very rare for a court to make an Order for **joint custody**. If parents are co-operating and want joint custody there's no *need* for a Court Order at all, even on divorce. Information has to be provided, regarding the arrangements for any children under 16, before the divorce will be granted; but the court doesn't have to make any specific Order about custody.

If there is no Court Order then parents retain the joint custody they always had.

Where parents cannot agree about the practicalities of arrangements for their children, and have to ask a court to make the decision, then the Sheriff deciding may feel there is not much chance of joint custody working, and may therefore not consider it.

13

COURT PROCEDURE

Most cases arising from family breakdown are dealt with in the local courts known as **Sheriff Courts**. There will be one in a town near you!

Cases, however, where there is a lot of money at stake, where questions of international law are involved, or where one party wishes to keep where they are living a secret, are often dealt with in the **Court of Session** in Edinburgh.

Which Court?

In a divorce action, the case can be dealt with in the Sheriff Court for the area in which either the husband or wife normally lives—the choice is for the one who starts the action. It will usually be the nearest court for convenience. Matters can be a bit more complicated if there have been recent quite dramatic shifts in address.

If only custody or the residence of children has to be decided, then usually the court near where the children are living has to be involved.

Where only financial support is involved, it can be the court near where the one wanting the money lives which makes the decision.

As you can begin to see, the rules about which court

deals with which action are very complicated—these are just the most general trends!

Procedure and Terminology

Since most cases are dealt with in the Sheriff Court, the terms used in the following discussion apply to the Sheriff Court rather than the Court of Session.

A divorce, or an action to do with children, starts off with a document called an **Initial Writ**. The person starting it is called the **Pursuer** and the other person is called the **Defender**.

This Writ states first of all what you are asking the court for—a divorce, Orders in relation to children, financial support or whatever—in short paragraphs called **craves**.

These are followed by a summary of the facts—the information on which you are basing these requests. Again these details are in numbered paragraphs, and are called **articles of condescendence**.

The Writ ends with statements of the legal rules you say should be used to get what you are asking for. These statements are called **pleas-in-law**.

The Writ will be signed by your solicitor as your Agent, and then sent to the court involved, asking for the court's authority—known as a **Warrant**—to intimate (**serve**) this on your partner.

Sometimes other people have to be told—for example, if the case involves Court Orders in relation to children, and your children are under supervision by the **Social Work Department**, the SWD will have to be sent a copy.

If you are saying that your partner has committed adultery, then the other person involved (known as the **Paramour**) will have a copy sent to them.

Court Orders relating to Children

☞ Previous Chapter

Interim Orders

☞ Chapter 17

If the action affects children, a copy should be sent to them. Sometimes the court decides that this is not appropriate, depending on their age, though practice varies from court to court. It's likely that a better way will be found to let the children know what's going on, in case they do have views to express regarding arrangements affecting them.

Usually **intimation** is made by your solicitor sending a copy of the Writ by Recorded Delivery post. If the person is not in when the postman tries to deliver the letter, or if the matter is particularly urgent, the copy is delivered by a person called a **Sheriff Officer**.

A period of time (the **period of notice**), normally **21 days**, is allowed for the person at the receiving end to decide if they want to oppose any of what is asked for. If they do, their solicitor will lodge a document known as a **Notice of Intention to Defend** and the case will become a **defended** (opposed) one.

Opposed Court Actions

☞ Next Chapter

If no opposition is lodged, the action is **undefended**, and usually the person starting the action will be given what they want by the court without any need for their attendance at court.

The court can give less money than is asked for, if the information provided by you doesn't seem to justify the amount requested. This is rare, however.

Where someone other than a biological parent is asking for custody, the Social Work Department is sent a copy of the Initial Writ and has to send a **background report** to the court. The **Sheriff** has to consider the report before granting custody, and could refuse if the report is unfavourable. Again, this doesn't often happen.

In **undefended** divorce actions, if there are children under 16 or any financial matters to be sorted out, the Sheriff has to have evidence from the person asking for the divorce and also from someone else. This evidence is usually given in sworn statements (**affidavits**), which can normally be signed in your solicitor's office.

Even if actions are not opposed, they usually take a few months from start to finish. As you can see, there's a lot of paperwork involved!

"So, Rover, which one do you want to live with?"

14

OPPOSED COURT ACTIONS

In January 1994, quite dramatic changes came into
effect concerning how disputed court actions should
proceed.

The new procedure retained many of the terms from
the previous procedure, but introduced a much stricter
timetable. If any of the requests (craves) are opposed
then a document known as a **Notice of Intention to
Defend** is sent to court within 21 days (the period of
notice) of the Initial Writ being intimated.

When the Notice of Intention to Defend arrives at
court, a date is fixed for you, your partner and the two
solicitors to attend court for what is called the **Options
Hearing**. The date will be just over three months from
when the action started. By then, you and your partner
will have had the chance to put in writing the main
points you wish to prove, or to have considered, before
a decision is made.

The Initial Writ is answered in a document
known as **Defences**. The Defences also set out any
requests, from whoever received the writ, regarding
financial claims or the arrangements for the children.
Once the Defences are available, you both have a
chance to amend your own written documents (known

as **Pleadings**) in response to the information provided by your partner.

There are very strict time limits for all these steps. There is also the possibility that a child affected by the action might become involved in the case directly. His or her solicitor will then set about submitting the necessary paperwork—or the Sheriff might decide that it would be best to appoint a **Curator**, usually a solicitor, to be involved in looking after the interests of the child or children.

If Legal Aid has to be applied for, the case will usually be held in abeyance while the application is processed. This delays things for several weeks, sometimes months. Such suspension of an action, without any date being set for it to recommence, is called a **sist** (which sounds like an annoying growth but is in fact totally passive!).

Generally, while your amendments to the written documents (pleadings) in court are being submitted, the negotiations between solicitors—and sometimes discussions between you and your partner—will be continuing.

If a settlement can be agreed, then everyone can heave a sigh of relief, and the details will be set out in a document known as a **Joint Minute**. This is signed by the solicitors and submitted to court. In most cases this will eliminate any need for you to go to court yourself.

In a divorce action, the sworn statements of evidence (affidavits) must be submitted to court before the court will make the Order, known as a **Decree**, divorcing you and detailing the terms of settlement.

In a minority of cases agreement is not reached, and the Sheriff has to make the decisions.

The Options Hearing

If there has been a sist, the original date for the Options Hearing will be delayed. Nevertheless, unless an agreement is reached, sooner or later you and your partner and the two solicitors will have to go to court for the Hearing. The Sheriff will have read your finalised written pleadings, and he or she will have to decide the next step.

Note, though, that the final decision is not made at the Options Hearing.

It's likely that the solicitors will do most of the talking at the Hearing, although the Sheriff may talk to you a little. This is a good opportunity for you to get the feel of being in court.

The next stage depends on what the Sheriff decides regarding the written pleadings. If your solicitor believes that your partner is making a request which is not justified, even if your partner's supporting statements can be proved, then a date is fixed for your solicitor to go into the matter more fully, in what is known as a **Debate**.

In family actions it is unusual for there to be Debates, but it is becoming more common because the legal rules are increasingly complicated.

Most disputed cases are dealt with at an event known as a **Proof**.

What Happens at a Proof?

A day (or sometimes longer) is fixed, several weeks in advance, for the Sheriff to hear evidence.

This requires that you, your partner and all your witnesses attend court in order to give the Sheriff the information you each have which has a bearing on the case *and which has been mentioned in the written pleadings*.

The Sheriff makes a decision based on what emerges at the Proof, not what is in the written pleadings, but you won't be allowed to bring up incidents or matters that have not been mentioned in writing. These rules are not stuck to quite as closely in family cases as in other types of court actions, but they do still apply.

When you give evidence, you are first asked questions by your own solicitor. These questions are not supposed to suggest an answer—they must not be **'leading'** questions. So don't be hurt if your solicitor asks you what your name is—it doesn't mean that they've forgotten, just that they're getting you into the way of answering non-leading questions!

After your solicitor has finished, your partner's solicitor can ask you questions. This is called **cross-examination**.

Leading questions *are* allowed at this stage. The idea of cross-examination is to allow your partner's solicitor to challenge and test what you have said, and also to ask you about things your partner wants to prove, in order to give you the chance to comment.

The same procedure applies for your witnesses, and in reverse for your partner, when it is your solicitor who carries out the cross-examination.

Once all the evidence has been presented, the solicitors sum up the main points and relate them to the law which applies. The Sheriff could decide then and there, but is more likely to want to think things over. This is known as taking the case to **avizandum**.

There will in most cases like this have been a Shorthand Writer taking down the evidence. Sometimes the Sheriff will ask for their notes to be typed out before making a decision.

The Sheriff's decision, which is called an **Interlocutor**, is normally quite long. It is sent to your solicitor who will 'translate' it for you.

TO THINK ABOUT

So much for the theory—what about the practice?

The written Pleadings and the Proof are not the place to offload your stockpiled frustration and annoyance—mud-slinging is strictly off-limits. Sheriffs are not there to referee a heated exchange of insults, but to hear evidence about facts—past, present and future—which are relevant to the legal rules.

You may feel really annoyed and upset by what your partner puts in the written pleadings. You may feel it is quite unfair or inaccurate. Remember that they probably feel the same way about what you have said. Try to keep calm, and don't worry if your partner has made statements you disagree with. If you deny something your partner has put in a written statement, then what they have written doesn't get them anywhere—*it still has to be proved.*

15

ATTENDANCE AT COURT

If you have to attend court to give evidence, remember you don't have to turn in an Oscar-winning performance! You're simply going there to provide information so as to let someone make a decision about a dispute in which you are involved. Just remember to speak clearly and answer the questions you're asked.

The first thing to do is to make sure you know where the court is!—the last thing you want is to be lost, late and panicking.

Be there in plenty of time. Court cases often don't start on time, but it is absolutely crucial that you are there just in case.

If you are going by car, find out about parking—not all courts have car parks.

When you arrive at the court building there should be a uniformed attendant about. Tell him the name of your case (*your* name) and he'll tell you where you should go.

You and your partner have the right to be in court throughout the case. However, witnesses who have not yet given evidence must not be in court when other people are giving their evidence. From this follows a very important point—once you have given your evidence, you must not talk about what has happened in court to any witnesses who have not yet given evidence.

Court Layout

In most courts the layout is essentially as shown below. Points to note are:

—The Sheriff sits on a raised part of the court, and the Shorthand Writer sits nearby.

—The Sheriff Clerk is there to deal with administrative matters at the beginning, but often will slip out during the case and only come back in at the end.

—The Bar Officer is the court official who will go out and call the witnesses.

—You and your partner sit at a table with your solicitors—except when you are giving evidence, when you go into the witness box.

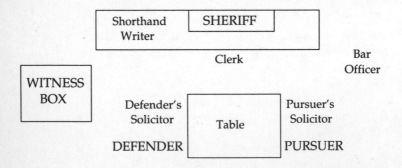

You will be put on oath. If you have any objection to this, you can ask to affirm instead.

Your solicitor has to do a great many things at once—ask questions, note answers, consider the balance of information, and mentally store important points for summing up—so certainly pass on briefly any information you may have that your lawyer doesn't, and which might be important, but try to be sure it's pretty vital!

Do remember, if the case goes on over lunch, that if you are with witnesses who have not yet given evidence *you must not discuss the case*. This may make conversation rather difficult, since the case will be the only thing on your mind, but it is very important to remember.

Don't pin your hopes on it all being over that day. Sometimes there's more business than the court can deal with, and the case might have to be set down for another day. Sometimes it takes longer than expected for the witnesses to give their information, and the case has to be finished at a later date.

Even if all the witnesses have finished and the solicitors have summed up, it is not very likely that the Sheriff will give his judgment at once. So calm and patience are the order of the day—quite a tall order too in the circumstances!

16

GROUNDS FOR DIVORCE

Most people know that divorces are granted because of the **irretrievable breakdown** of their marriage. What is less widely known is that there are only certain ways you can prove the fact that there has been an irretrievable breakdown.

IF YOU HAVE BEEN LIVING APART
FOR LESS THAN TWO YEARS

If you want a divorce within the first two years you live apart, or if you are still living together, you have to prove that your partner has **behaved unreasonably** or has committed **adultery**.

Unreasonable Behaviour

This is much wider than the old grounds of cruelty which it replaces. It includes physical violence but extends to habitual drinking, verbal abuse, irresponsible or callous behaviour, and a wide range of human activity which might be acceptable to some couples but is considered objectively by the court to be 'off-limits'.

Adultery

You must be able to prove your partner has had a sexual relationship with someone else. While you're not expected to have eye witnesses available, there does have to be clear circumstantial evidence, often backed up by an admission.

Note that an admission on its own is not enough. It is possible to use evidence from your partner but there has to be another witness as well. Sometimes the partner and paramour might co-operate to provide the necessary affidavits, but not all Sheriffs would accept this as sufficient evidence.

Sometimes a Private Investigator is involved in gathering evidence. This is not by way of hiding in the wardrobe with a camera—the Investigator might keep watch for a time, but would rarely do so extensively because of the cost involved.

In most cases the Investigator gathers evidence from observation, and then goes to the door and tackles the couple about their relationship.

Quite often the couple are prepared to admit about their relationship to the Private Investigator.

IF YOU HAVE BEEN LIVING APART
FOR MORE THAN TWO YEARS

Two-Year Separation With Consent

Well, this is fairly self-explanatory! If there is a period of non-cohabitation lasting for **two years**, and you and your partner both want a divorce, then this is the most civilised way of establishing your right to end the marriage.

The non-cohabitation starts whenever you and your husband separate—there's no need to go through any formal steps at the time, so long as you have a note of the date.

If there are children under 16, or if the court is going to have to sort out any money matters in the divorce, then you will need an independent witness who can confirm the period of separation from their own knowledge.

In any divorce on these grounds, both you and your partner need to be involved, one to ask the court for the divorce and the other to consent, so it's very important to keep in touch regarding any change of address.

It is possible to have the period of non-cohabitation taking place under the same roof, but as you may imagine this is not easy to achieve! You would have to live totally separate lives—not just separate beds but also separate cooking, eating, cleaning and socialising arrangements. It is unusual to find this type of non-cohabitation.

Five-Year Separation

If you and your partner live apart for **five years** you can use these grounds, even if your partner doesn't want a divorce.

In fact, you can apply for a divorce on these grounds even if you don't know where your partner is, although in that case intimation may have to be made to other people.

The only way the divorce could be stopped is by your partner proving that divorce would cause grave financial hardship. However, because of the financial provision which can be made on divorce, it is virtually unheard of for a divorce to be refused on these grounds.

Desertion

The remaining way of proving irretrievable breakdown is **desertion**—but an action can only be raised on these grounds after two years have gone by and it is not a very common reason for divorce.

In order to use these grounds, you have to have wanted to stay together at the time your partner left.

"So that's 4 years, 364 days, 23 hours and—"
"Hi, honey, I'm home!"

Simplified Divorce Procedure

If, and *only* if:
—You have no children under 16, **and**
—There are no financial matters to sort out in the divorce, **and**
—You have been separated for two years, **and**
—You both want a divorce,

or:

—You have been separated for five years, **and**
—Your partner doesn't claim the divorce would cause severe financial hardship,

then you can use the so called **'quickie'** divorce procedure.

This involves getting the appropriate form from the local Sheriff Court, after you have been separated for at least two years. The form has quite clear instructions explaining how it should be completed. If you are seeking a 'two-year' divorce your partner has to sign. There is also a part which you have to sign in front of someone authorised to administer oaths, such as a Justice of the Peace or a Notary Public. You don't need to use a solicitor, though you can if you choose.

Advice &
Assistance

p101

If you are on a low income you might qualify under the Legal Aid **Advice & Assistance** scheme, in which case you would be exempt from paying the court fee.

Change of Name

If you want to go back to using your original name you don't need to wait until you're divorced. Equally you can go on using your married name after the divorce.

If you have children they can continue to use your

58

married name or change to your original name. If the other parent objects, this might be something the court would be asked to decide as a specific issue, when the relevant part of the Children (Scotland) Act comes into force (probably in November 1996).

While there are ways to have a change of name recorded by the Registrar General, you can change a name without having to follow any special procedures, simply by using it consistently.

IN SUMMARY

You don't have to have been separated for two years before you start a divorce, if you can prove that your partner has behaved unreasonably or has committed adultery.

In fact you don't even have to be separated at all to start divorce proceedings. If you can prove adultery or unreasonable behaviour, and give a satisfactory reason for remaining under the same roof as your partner (housing difficulties, for example), then you should be able to get your divorce.

It would be a matter of having evidence to prove that the marriage is over, and that you have not accepted (**condoned**) your partner's behaviour.

If neither adultery nor unreasonable behaviour applies, then a separation of two years is needed before a divorce will be granted.

If the separation is of between two and five years' duration, your partner's consent is also required, but their consent is not necessary if you have been apart for at least five years.

17

INTERIM ORDERS

To reach the end of a court action, and arrive at a final decision, takes a long time—several months at least, and occasionally years.

Often in family actions a crisis blows up and it becomes essential to have some aspect or other decided at short notice. In this case it is possible to ask the court to make an **Interim Order**.

An Interim Order is made before all the facts are established. Often the written information available is very brief. Nevertheless, the decision at this stage can often be very important in influencing the final outcome. It is very difficult to appeal successfully against an Interim Order, so it's important to take them seriously!

The most common requests for Interim Orders in family actions are for an Interim Interdict, an Interim Exclusion Order, Interim Custody, Interim Access or Interim Aliment.

When the provisions of the Children (Scotland) Act concerning Residence and Contact Orders come into effect (probably in November 1996), Interim Custody and Access will give way to new Orders under the Act.

The changes are further discussed in Chapter 12

☞ p39

Interim Interdict

If your partner has been abusive, and you think it might happen again, you can ask the court to grant you a **Protective Order** which is usually worded to stop '**molestation**' (though going into more detail than that).

If your partner has threatened to snatch your children, or smash up or sell your furniture, or all of these things, you can ask for an Order to prevent this.

Your solicitor frames the written request, in all the examples just given, so as to try to persuade the Sheriff to grant the Order before your partner is told about it.

If you are not married, or you are married but not living in the matrimonial home, then you can ask the court for an Interim Interdict to keep your partner away from where you are living. A copy of the Order has to be brought to your partner's notice, usually by a Sheriff Officer handing it over.

If you are married you can ask the court to add a **Power of Arrest** to your Interim Interdict, but this can only be done at a Hearing that your partner is given the opportunity of attending (or of having a solicitor attending on their behalf).

Interim Exclusion Order

If your partner's behaviour is violent, or so abusive or intimidating that it is affecting your or your children's health, you can ask for an **Interim Exclusion Order** to keep your partner out of the matrimonial home.

If you are not married, and the house you share is

Exclusion Orders and occupancy rights are both discussed in greater detail in Chapter 10

owned or rented by your partner, you can only get an Exclusion Order if you have asked the court for and been granted occupancy rights.

With married couples an Interim Exclusion Order can be requested at the same time as a divorce action is started. On the other hand, it is quite possible to ask for an Exclusion Order on its own—not as part of a divorce action. You should in any case get a Power of Arrest at the same time as the Exclusion Order.

It is important to remember that if you get an Interim Exclusion Order when you begin a divorce action, then once the divorce is granted the Exclusion Order stops. This is because once you are no longer married the house is no longer a matrimonial home.

Power of Arrest

This Power can be attached to Interdicts granted only where a couple are married*, and to Exclusion Orders. It only takes effect if copies of all the correct papers are sent to the police. Your solicitor attends to that.

The Power of Arrest gives the police the power to arrest someone who appears to be acting in breach of the relevant Court Order it is attached to. This means that they could take someone away just for turning up outside the matrimonial home, although in practice there would normally have to be a considerable row before they would do so.

If your partner is arrested because he has turned up in defiance of an Exclusion Order, he isn't kept in jail

* Unless an unmarried partner who has an Interdict also has an Occupancy Order as outlined in Chapter 10 (which is quite unusual).

indefinitely. In most cases he will be released the next day, although in some circumstances he could be kept in a little longer.

Whatever happened at your house might then lead to a criminal prosecution against your partner, or alternatively your solicitor could start a Breach of Interdict action.

Breach of Court Orders

☞ p66

It's important to remember that as soon as a divorce is granted then any Power of Arrest no longer applies.

Interim Orders Concerning Children

If the children are with you, and you have good reason to think your partner is likely to try to change this, you can ask the court to give you an Interim Order to keep things the same until a final decision is made.

Court Orders relating to children are also discussed in Chapter 12

If the children are not with you, and you have good reasons why they should be, you can ask the court to give you an **Interim Custody** (or **Residence**) **Order** requiring that the children be based with you. You will need much better reasons in order to persuade the court in this case. Where the children are living with one parent, then to change that during a court action—before all the different stages are gone through and all the evidence is available—requires very strong justification. Evidence of abuse against the children or totally inadequate housing are possibilities.

You do have to keep in mind that once you start lobbing accusations about, this will cause a great deal of anger which in turn will probably affect the children either directly or indirectly.

You have to be pretty sure of your ground—**be especially careful not to overreact to what the children say to you**. Children usually want both their parents to be back under the same roof. This can lead them to say to both parents separately that they want to live with the one they are talking to at the time.

This should be a signal to make arrangements to give the children the greatest possible contribution from you both, not to fight over them—**they need you both!**

If you are having trouble seeing your children, you can ask for an **Interim Access** (or **Contact**) **Order**. Orders made through the court have to be very specific and are rather inflexible, so it is always better to sort out arrangements directly with your partner if at all possible. If, though, this is simply impossible to achieve, then it can relieve some of the pressure if a Court Order is made.

Rather than simply deciding on the information each solicitor is putting forward, the court has two other options.

One is to make a formal referral to mediation. This involves both parents having to make contact with a Mediation Service, in the hope that both will agree to attend a joint meeting with a mediator to see if things might be worked out by negotiation, even at this stage.

The other possibility is to ask for a background report from either a social worker or a solicitor, who will visit both parents and make whatever enquiries they feel necessary.

The information in the report will help the Sheriff decide.

The court might also be asked to decide a more specific question, about matters such as health or education, in an **Interim (Specific Issues) Order**.

Interim Aliment

If you want financial support for yourself during the course of the action then you should ask for **Interim Aliment**.

Since April 1993 support for children in most cases is dealt with by the **Child Support Agency**, though there will still be some circumstances in which the court has to decide.

Where the court is to decide, it is important that you provide as much detail as possible about your income and expenditure. It's helpful to have receipts for as many things as you can. Your partner should respond with the same sort of information.

Procedure at an Interim Hearing

Quite often requests for Interim Orders are dealt with by the Sheriff in his or her room rather than in the courtroom.

This is known as a **Hearing in Chambers.**

In that case you're not very likely to be involved in the Hearing itself—your solicitor will explain the important points to the Sheriff for you.

Since the outcome of the Hearing is likely to be very important, you might want to be in the court building anyway—you could then hear the decision straight away. Also, if something came up at the last minute your solicitor would be able to discuss it with you. It's a good idea to discuss with your solicitor whether you should be there.

Sometimes interim requests (known as **Interim Motions**) are considered with a number of other cases in the courtroom. The cases are read out from a list (known as a **roll**) and the solicitors involved stand up and say their piece. You can sit in the courtroom and listen to what's going on.

Usually the Sheriff makes a decision about all interim requests then and there, though occasionally another date might be fixed if a report is ordered or if the parents are referred to mediation.

Other Interim Requests

In family actions there are quite a number of other requests your solicitor might make to the court on your behalf during the course of the case.

You can ask for information about your partner's money or business. You can ask for money which has to be spent on the family home to be apportioned. You can ask for assets like a house or pension scheme to be valued.

Bear in mind, though, that some of these steps might be rather expensive.

Breach of Court Orders

If your partner disobeys a Court Order, you can ask the court to fix a date when your partner must appear and say whether they accept that they are in breach of the Court Order.

If your partner denies the breach, another date will be fixed for the court to hear evidence. You have to be able to prove that the breach occurred.

If your partner admits the breach, or if it is proved, the court can fine or imprison them. The imposition of some penalty, usually a fine, is likely if the breach involves violence. Conversely, if the problem relates to arrangements for children the Sheriff is more likely to tackle it in such a way as to get the arrangements working.

18

DIVISION OF MONEY AND PROPERTY

(1)—MARRIED COUPLES

One of the big worries after separation is money. Two households are going to be more expensive than one. There may be debt already, and even if there isn't, there is a real risk that some will start mounting up unless you're both able to be realistic.

There are two separate money issues to tackle.

One is the question of the ongoing finances, including weekly or monthly support, division of responsibility for existing debt, and commitments like Building Society repayments, insurance premiums and suchlike.

The other is how to split up fairly the property that you have built up during the marriage (known as **matrimonial property**).

It is possible to ask the court to sort out the ongoing finances at any time, but it is generally only in a divorce action that you can force a decision regarding the division of matrimonial property.

In practice couples often want to sort out both of

Separation
Agreements

👉 Chapter
8

Mediation

👉 Chapter
7

these aspects as soon as possible, even if they're not launching into a divorce action at once. Your solicitor can help you to negotiate a Separation Agreement taking into account the rules that would apply on divorce. You could use mediation for part of the process.

The two areas—ongoing finances and the division of matrimonial property—tend to be bound up with one another. This is particularly so with what is often the key question: what is to happen to the family home, if it is owned? What income each of you will be left with will be the main factor in deciding who, if either, could afford to keep up the repayments to the Building Society.

So, as you can see, you can't really take anything in isolation.

What Is Matrimonial Property?

Matrimonial property is all the property belonging to you both at the time you separate or raise a divorce action (whichever is earlier) and which you acquired during the marriage (or any house or furniture you bought before then to use as or for a family home), including any business interests either of you built up after you married but before you separated.

It includes the proportion of *pension* or *life policy* interests which accumulated during the time you were married and lived together. It excludes *inherited money* and *personal gifts* from third parties.

Having said this, it must be pointed out that the question of whether or not a particular asset counts as matrimonial property is not always clear-cut, and courts will decide each case on its own merits.

Division of Matrimonial Property

A few years ago a new law was introduced to set out the rules regarding the financial side of divorce.

The new law, **The Family Law (Scotland) Act 1985**, tried to encourage the 'clean break' principle. Lump sum payments, known as **capital sums**, were hoped to take the place of ongoing payments to a former partner, and the circumstances in which the ongoing support would be payable were restricted.

In addition it was recognised that one partner in a marriage often earned less, but contributed more to caring for the children or running the household, and in so doing might have given up career prospects.

It was decided that both the financial and non-financial contributions should be acknowledged. Economic imbalances were generally to be evened up. In reality this has proved difficult, because there is often simply not enough money available.

The basic principle set out in the Family Law Act is that the net value of matrimonial property should be shared fairly between you. 'Fairly' usually means equally, unless special circumstances justify a different apportionment.

That may sound reasonably straightforward. It was certainly intended to give a clear framework for sorting out the family finances at the end of a marriage. Unfortunately it's turned out to be rather murky in practice!

One overriding principle is that although the way someone behaved might be the reason the divorce itself is granted, that behaviour will usually not be taken into account when the money side is considered.

You might be surprised by this. You might think, for example, that your partner should be penalised for having walked out on you to go and live with someone else. It is perhaps not easy to accept, but it's important to realise that even though the divorce action may be fault-based the financial division will not be.

It is only in very restricted circumstances that conduct during the marriage can be taken into account. The cases where this is a factor are very rare.

The other general point to remember is that if the financial side of things had to be sorted out in court rather than by agreement it doesn't matter which of you raises the action, the other one can normally get their entitlement sorted out in the same action.

Looking at the division of matrimonial property in practice, the simplest case would be that of a couple who have both worked at similar jobs, have no children, have a car each, and bought a house with a Building Society loan.

They would have similar pension interests and so that aspect could be disregarded. If their cars were of similar values they could each keep a car. If all the household contents were bought for or during the marriage, they could agree a division that would give each half the value. The house could be sold, the loan paid off, and the proceeds after clearing the expenses of sale could be split equally. There would be no question of ongoing financial support.

Of course, only a tiny proportion of couples are like this; the vast majority of you lead much more complicated lives!

THE GREY AREAS

Pension Interests

Pensions have proved one of the most dramatic elements in the new law. The value of the pension interests which actuaries have assessed in fairly long-lasting marriages has been very substantial, particularly in some areas of employment.

The Fire service and the Police force, for example, have both yielded valuations which make the pension interests a significant part of the matrimonial property, often as valuable as the money tied up in the family home, sometimes even more valuable. These pension interests are often not going to produce any actual cash for years to come, but the general idea is to have the share-out of the matrimonial property now.

This has posed something of a dilemma for the courts. If there is a substantial amount of money tied up in the matrimonial home, it is easier to sort things out by either transferring or selling the house, and by then giving the lion's share of the proceeds to the one without the pension interests.

Generally, the trend at the beginning seemed to be to give the partner without the pension interests two fifths rather than one half of their value, either as a cash sum or by transfer of the matrimonial home. That trend became rather diluted in later court decisions, which took a variety of approaches from giving half of the value to not giving any share of pension interests at all. Giving no share was in quite unusual circumstances, but it does highlight how wide the range of decisions is.

There has also developed at the same time a lively debate about how pension interests should be valued.

The position at the moment is that it is impossible to predict how a court would go about putting a value on pension interests, but that realistic account should be taken of them.

There will be a new possibility soon. One of the provisions of the **Pensions Act 1995** is to allow part of lump sum pension benefits to be earmarked by the court for providing a capital sum. This provision should come into force during 1996.

However, since the money isn't paid until the person retires, the provision is rather at odds with the idea of the 'clean break'.

If the person entitled to the pension dies before the retirement date for that scheme, it is possible that no lump sum will be paid out, and so there would be no money for a capital sum. In a way this could be seen as fair, because the pension would have turned out to be of little value after all.

Earmarking would be useful if the pension is the only asset. If there are other assets, especially if there is a house, it might still be preferable to sort things out by transferring the other assets.

If you do decide on earmarking, then it seems that the court will have to be asked to include that provision in the divorce. It probably won't be possible just to have it as part of a Separation Agreement.

The Matrimonial Home

If one of you owned what became the family home before the marriage, or if it was bought with money one of you inherited or received as a personal gift, working out how it fits into the matrimonial jigsaw becomes more complicated.

Similarly, if the house was bought jointly but there

has been a long period of separation before a financial settlement is arranged, there is no clear-cut rule governing what is to be done about any increase in value since separation.

The court cases which have touched on these matters are not providing a clear guiding principle.

Financial Support

Quite apart from division of matrimonial property, there is the question of the possible need for *ongoing financial support*.

While you are still married, if you are not working or are earning much less than your partner, you can ask for weekly or monthly support called **aliment**—in this case it is called **spousal aliment**, since it is for yourself, and is separate from support for any children you might have.

However, if your partner wants you to live with him or her, and if this offer is reasonable, you may not be able to get aliment for yourself.

The amount of aliment has to take into account the needs and resources of both parties. The level of aliment is another unpredictable thing!

To continue receiving ongoing financial support *after divorce* (this time called **periodical allowance**) you must:

—Be hampered from being self-supporting because of looking after any children of the marriage who are under 16.

In this case the support can continue for as long as the restriction is there. Note, though, it is harder to prove that it is the children who are the limiting factor the older they get.

or:

—Have been substantially dependent on your partner for financial support.

In this category you can only have a claim for up to three years after the divorce.

or:

—Be likely to suffer serious financial hardship as a result of the divorce.

It is very difficult to qualify under this heading, but if you do then the length of the award is not restricted to three years. It can be fixed for as long as the court is persuaded is reasonable. However, it is very unusual, even in this category, to have an award of financial support without a cut-off date.

If you want to claim periodical allowance, you have to show that your partner can't pay you a lump sum instead. In practice this may not be too much of a hurdle—it is quite rare for anyone to have enough capital to settle a claim straight away.

Sometimes the fact that a claim could be made for periodical allowance can be used to justify, as an alternative, the transfer of the family home—even if such a transfer would appear to result in an unfair split, having regard only to the total matrimonial property at the time of divorce.

Subsequent Variation of Aliment
or Periodical Allowance

If either of you undergoes a major change in circumstances, you can ask the court to review the level of financial support.

The overall amount of a capital sum on the other hand can't be changed, even if it's being paid by instalments.

"You will write, Rover . . . ?"

TO THINK ABOUT

Even if something is bought during the time a couple have been married and living together (which brings it under the heading of matrimonial property), if it was bought mainly using money that definitely wasn't matrimonial property (such as inherited money) then the court may choose not to include it when deciding the financial split.

One of the problems is that each court case is being decided on the basis of its own particular facts. This means that there are few clear, predictable rules.

It is always worth remembering that the cost of having the financial split sorted out in court is liable to use up quite a chunk of the resources available, especially if there are numerous expert witnesses like surveyors and actuaries involved! It is better if you can keep the principle of fair sharing in mind and reach an agreement which you can both live with!

The division of the property side is usually settled either by the award of a lump sum (a **capital payment**), or by the transfer of property, or by a mixture of both. The Family Law Act did allow for the possibility of capital payments being paid by instalments. This certainly conflicts with the 'clean break' principle, but so do many other of the harsh realities of life—such as children!

19

DIVISION OF MONEY AND PROPERTY

(2)—UNMARRIED COUPLES

If you are not married, ownership of whatever you have accumulated along the way will depend on which of you paid for each item.

If the house you have lived in belongs to your partner, you can ask the court to let you stay on for a while. However, you cannot ask for a share of its value simply because you and your partner have been living there together.

Occupancy Rights

p32

If your partner rents the house, there are some circumstances in which you could have the tenancy transferred, but anything that is owned by one or other of you stays that way after separation.

Transfer of Tenancy

☞ p32

This does make it very important to think through what you are doing if you start living with someone.

In some circumstances you could make a claim based on what you have contributed during a relationship with the idea that things were to be joint. However, this is an area where there aren't many cases to show the way, and quite a few hurdles have to be jumped.

You can't ask for ongoing financial support for yourself, even if you are not working and your former partner is.

On the other hand, financial support is obtainable for children—if you have children then both of you have responsibilities for the financial costs, in the same way as married couples have.

☞ Next Chapter

TO THINK ABOUT

Marriage does give a lot of automatic rights now concerning sharing things at the end of a relationship.

Sometimes people think that if you live together for a long time then you become a '**common law**' husband and wife. It is terribly unusual to be able to prove a marriage this way. You have to be able to persuade a court that people thought you were actually married, and that for quite a long time you have been behaving as if you had gone through a marriage ceremony—for example calling yourselves 'Mr and Mrs'. Most couples who live together nowadays are quite open about the fact that they are not married.

20

FINANCIAL SUPPORT FOR CHILDREN

Both married and unmarried parents, and in some circumstances people who have been like parents to a child, can be asked to share the financial responsibilities of child care.

If you are not living with the children, this is usually in the form of weekly or monthly support called **aliment** or **child maintenance**.

The rules that give guidance on how much the aliment should be are quite general, whether you are dealing with the matter between you or having the court fix an amount. It depends on the needs and resources of all concerned.

The trouble is that in most households the needs for fairly basic things are at least as much as (and quite often more than!) the resources for that household alone. Thus the arithmetic suggests that no aliment can be afforded, whereas the reality demands that it must be! The financial cake of those who are working is being divided into so many pieces that there are only crumbs to go round!

The **Child Support Agency** (since April 1993) applies a formula to work out how much maintenance should be paid by the absent partner for children. If the person looking after the child is receiving **Income Support**, **Family Credit** or **Disability Working Allowance**, the Child Support Agency will apply the formula and recover the appropriate amount from the other parent. It will be only in really unusual circumstances that the Agency would not do this.

For details of the CSA formula

☞ Chapter 23

The Agency can be used on a voluntary basis if there is no existing Agreement or Court Order, even when there is no payment of Benefit.

Existing Court Orders relating to child maintenance will continue in force, although the court can alter these if there is a change in circumstances.

At some point the Child Support Agency will regulate most child maintenance Orders where parties are unable to come to a voluntary agreement, even if there is an existing Court Order or Agreement. However, the courts will still deal with fixing the level of financial support under the following headings:

If You Have Accepted a Child into Your Family

If you have taken on the parental role towards a child or children, and treated them as if they were your family, then you may be asked to provide financially for them by the person caring for them.

This means that a step-parent can be asked for financial support after a separation.

If Your Children Are 18 or Over & Under 25

If your children are over 18 but still under 25 they can ask you for financial support if they are still in full-time education or training.

The education or training must be reasonable. It is

unlikely that a court would expect you to finance seven unsuccessful attempts to get standard grades nor, at the other extreme, a succession of increasingly academic and impractical qualifications.

(The Child Support Agency can deal with children under 19 still receiving full-time education in some cases.)

School Fees

If your children are at a private school, the Child Support Agency formula won't allow for payment of fees. You would therefore still have to ask the court to sort this out if it can't be arranged between you.

High Earners

If either or both of you have a very high income, the Child Support Agency formula may come up with an amount of aliment that doesn't really reflect the needs and resources of all concerned.

The Agency will set a maximum amount where agreement cannot be reached, and only once an assessment is made can application be made to the court to 'top up' this sum.

Disabled Children

Extra costs for some disabled children will have to be fixed by the courts if a figure can't be agreed.

21

APPEALING TO A TRIBUNAL

Many separated people receive State Benefit of some
sort. **Income Support** or **Family Credit** are the most
common, but if all the upheaval of a separation
leads to loss of employment then the question of
entitlement to **Unemployment Benefit** may arise.
(The conditions for receipt of this Benefit will change
during 1996, and it will be renamed **Jobseekers'
Allowance**.)

Additionally, a considerable number of separated
parents will be affected by the decisions of the Child
Support Agency.

Any decision on a claim to Benefit should be in
writing. If you don't agree with a decision about your
Benefit or an assessment by the Child Support Agency
then you can appeal against it.

When you receive the decision you should be told
exactly how to appeal. Your appeal will be decided by
either a **Social Security Appeal Tribunal** or a **Child
Support Agency Appeal Tribunal**.

In both cases the Tribunal is made up of three people:
one is a lawyer and the other two are people who have
a knowledge of local circumstances and training in the
rules and regulations.

The Tribunal is quite independent from the Department which made the decision. It is much more informal than a court, and you do not need anyone to represent you. There is no cost involved in appealing, and the Tribunal will help you explain your case.

Why Should I Appeal?

You can appeal against any decision in which you believe the regulations have not been applied correctly or in which the wrong facts have been considered by the person who made the decision.

Quite often you won't know very much about the regulations. You can ask for help from your local Citizens' Advice Bureau or welfare rights officer, or from a solicitor who deals with such issues. Alternatively, if you think you have a good reason for disagreeing with the decision, you can simply put that reason in your letter of appeal.

You should say why you think the decision is wrong rather than just say 'I appeal', especially in Child Support Agency appeals since there is an opportunity for the Agency to reconsider the decision before the matter goes to appeal.

The following are examples of circumstances in which appeals relating to Benefits may arise. Appealing against Child Support Agency decisions is discussed in detail later.

CSA Appeals
☞ p98

Income Support

CSA Assess-
ments versus
Maintenance
Payments
☞ p85

There is much less discretion in the Income Support system than there was before 1988 when it was called Supplementary Benefit, but there are still some points which might be argued over.

The present Benefit system is not designed to meet the individual needs of claimants, but is based on flat rate payments with the addition of premiums where there are certain conditions.

Cohabitation

If you are getting Income Support, and you have a regular partner who is either working or claiming Benefit from a different address, then a question might arise regarding whether you are actually living together as husband and wife.

If the Benefits Agency believe they can prove you are, they may stop your Benefit and might ask for money back that you have already been paid.

If you appeal against this, it is up to the Benefits Agency to prove the cohabitation. There would have to be much more than an occasional overnight stay. The relationship should be more like that of a married couple, with shared accommodation and responsibilities.

Quite often these questions arise because someone telephones the Benefits Agency anonymously to clype!—but random home visits are now carried out on a sample of claims.

Sometimes accusations are merely malicious, but it may be that people have drifted into more settled cohabitation without thinking of the consequences on their Benefit. In other cases, those claiming are trying to work the system by retaining separate claims, or by not telling the department when there is a change in their lifestyle.

If people knowingly claim Benefit when they shouldn't it can lead to a criminal prosecution, so it is very important to report any change of circumstances to the Benefits Agency.

If you are involved in an appeal about cohabitation, it is helpful to have as much proof as possible to confirm that you are living apart. So, for example, it would be most useful if your partner could come along, and if you had something such as a letter from someone living at your partner's address confirming how long your partner has been there.

However, even if that is not possible, it is still worth going along yourself.

As well as the time you do spend together the Tribunal will be interested in knowing if you have any children from the relationship, and if you pool your money. It is features such as these that suggest cohabitation.

Note, though, that these appeals can be difficult, and you would be better to seek advice.

Maintenance Payments

Problems can arise if you are given money by your ex-partner when you are on Benefit. You should report such payments, and an equal amount will then be taken off your Income Support. The situation can get rather muddled if your ex-partner sometimes pays and sometimes doesn't. On the other hand, if your ex-partner buys clothes or other things for the children, this does not count as income for you.

Once a Child Support Agency assessment is in operation, the Agency will arrange for the money to be paid over by your partner directly. In some circumstances you can arrange for the money to be collected by the Child Support Agency and paid by them to you—this makes it easier for the Agency to monitor payments.

You would still have to report if for some reason your ex-partner gave you extra money. If you do not report receiving such money you may lose your entitlement to it.

Money from Work

If you start work and don't tell the Benefits Agency, again you are liable to be asked to repay money paid by way of Benefit for any period you were working, regardless of when you received your pay.

If you deny receiving the money, or if you disagree with the amount claimed back, you can appeal and say why.

Family Credit

If you have claimed Family Credit then you might disagree with the way your income has been calculated—especially if you are self-employed!

If you do disagree, then you have to provide as much information as possible about your financial situation. There are rules regarding how your income is calculated. These do not take into account unusually high or low wages, but do include overtime.

Remember that you can apply for Family Credit if you are working 16 hours a week or more and are looking after one or more children.

Unemployment Benefit

If you find that as a result of the separation you have to give up work, you might find yourself without Unemployment Benefit and receiving less Income Support than you normally would.

Where someone chooses to give up work without what the Benefits Agency consider to be a good reason, Unemployment Benefit can be withheld for up to 6 months. While your Unemployment Benefit is being withheld, your Income Support is automatically cut, except in limited circumstances.

What constitutes 'a good reason' is not defined, and it is important to explain the background fully to your employer if you leave, and to the Benefits Agency if they ask.

If Unemployment Benefit is refused for this reason and you disagree, it is very important to appeal against *that* decision—sometimes people appeal against the cut in Income Support, when what they really want to argue against is the refusal of Unemployment Benefit.

In an appeal of this kind, if you succeed the Tribunal can either award you Unemployment Benefit from the date of your claim, or they could reduce the length of time for which it is refused.

Very similar rules will apply to Jobseekers' Allowance, when this comes into force during 1996.

22

TRIBUNAL PROCEDURE

Tribunals are held in a variety of different venues—including Church Halls. No Social Security Appeal Tribunals or Child Support Appeal Tribunals are held in court, and most are in prominent, specially designated premises.

After you have written to the appropriate department to say why you disagree with their decision, you will receive papers about your appeal from the Tribunal office. You will also receive a booklet from the Independent Appeals Service: *APPEALS! What to expect from our service.*

Notification of the time and place when your appeal will be heard may be sent separately, but you will receive at least 10 days' notice.

The papers will explain in much greater detail how the decision was made, and the rules and regulations will be set out. However, it is not always easy to understand these papers. It might therefore be a good idea to go to a Citizens' Advice Bureau, a welfare rights officer, or a Solicitor who deals with Benefit cases. They could go over the papers with you, and either come to the Tribunal with you or give you a written statement of the points which you want to make.

The main thing is to try to be there yourself. The appeal can be heard without you, but it is much better for you to go along. An appeal is much more likely to succeed if the person who is appealing attends the Tribunal personally.

When you arrive at the Tribunal's premises you will be shown where the Tribunal waiting room is. You should take a seat, and quite soon a Tribunal Officer called a **Clerk** will come and have a word with you. The Clerk will sort out expenses and explain what happens next. After a time (often not very long), you will be asked to go in to the Tribunal room.

The three Tribunal members will be sitting on one side of a table and you will be invited to sit opposite. There will in addition be someone there from the department involved, called the **Presenting Officer**. The Clerk will also be in the room for most of the time.

In Child Support Agency cases the other parent may also be there, although you will not have to wait beforehand in the same room.

The Chairman will introduce everyone, and then your appeal papers will be referred to and as much information as is needed will be gathered in by the Tribunal members from you and the Presenting Officer. The Tribunal members will want to put you at your ease and help you to explain all that is important.

If you have any papers bring them along and they can be looked at. You can bring a witness along if you feel that would be helpful to your case.

You and the Presenting Officer will then be asked to step outside again while the Tribunal reach their decision. You will almost always be asked back into the Tribunal room, and told the decision. Tribunals are encouraged to give their decision on the day. In any event you will receive a written decision in the post in a few weeks.

So do remember, Tribunals want to meet you and hear what you have to say. They know that the rules and regulations will probably seem very complicated to you. These rules *are* very complicated!—you are not expected to understand all the ins and outs, just to explain your circumstances and why *you* think the decision was wrong.

23

CHILD SUPPORT AGENCY

Since April 1993 financial support for children from the parent not living with them may be fixed and collected by the Child Support Agency.

Parents who have the children based with them and who receive Benefit will be expected to seek a maintenance assessment from the other parent (known as the **'absent partner'**). Failure to co-operate may result in a reduction in Benefit.

If you are looking after the children, and receiving Income Support, Family Credit or Disability Working Allowance, then this service will be free. Otherwise a fee will usually be payable, although payment of fees is suspended from April 1995 to April 1997.

The amount of maintenance is fixed by using a rather complicated formula. To work out the amount you need to know the figures used to calculate entitlement to Income Support—even if neither of you is on Income Support. These figures usually change in April of every year. You can ask for a leaflet showing the rates in force at any time from the Benefits Agency.

The Formula

It is possible to work out child maintenance on the basis of the statutory formula, but often it is difficult to be certain of all the information needed. The following gives an outline of how the formula is calculated. There are three stages:

1) The **Maintenance Requirement** for the 'qualifying child or children' has to be worked out. To do this,

    add:
    a) The Income Support age-related allowance for each child.

    b) The Income Support family premium.

    c) If the youngest qualifying child is under 11—
        The full Income Support allowance for a lone adult over 24, **or**
        If the youngest qualifying child is 11 to 13—
        75% of that allowance, **or**
        If the youngest child is 14 to 16—
        50% of that allowance, **or**
        If the youngest child is 16 or over—
        the adult personal allowance is not included.

    d) If the carer is a lone parent—
        the Income Support lone parent premium.

    then **subtract:**
    the Child Benefit for the children.

2) The **Assessable Income** of **each parent** has to be worked out. Note that if a parent is on Income Support, or is on a very low wage, their Assessable Income will be zero.

Start by calculating the **Basic Net Income**.
This is usually the average take home pay of the employed, and the equivalent of that for the self-employed, subtracting half of any pension contributions, but income from other sources may also be included. Child Benefit is not included at this stage.

From this, **subtract** the **Exempt Income:**
  a) the Income Support allowance for a lone adult over 24, **and**
  b) reasonable housing costs. (It is important to realise that 'reasonable' can be as much as half someone's income, but money paid to a close relative for digs will not be allowed as housing costs.)

3) The **assessment calculation** can then be tackled.

The maintenance assessment is made against the parent who doesn't live with the children—the **'absent parent'**. The parent with whom the children live will not be ordered to pay themselves anything!— but their income will affect the total maintenance assessment. Both parents' Assessable Income is taken into account when working out what the absent parent has to pay, as the liability is in proportion to the Assessable Income of each.

a) The **Basic Element:**

After revisals to the formula, the absent parent may be asked to pay up to 30% of their Assessable Income in order to satisfy their share of the children's Maintenance Requirement.

Up to 33% of the Assessable Income may be payable where there are arrears of maintenance.

Remember, the amount the absent parent is expected to contribute is affected by any Assessable Income of the other parent.

b) The **Additional Element:**

If the Maintenance Requirement is met by the basic element, and the absent parent still has some Assessable Income, then a proportion of this will be included in the calculation.

c) **Protected Income:**

The assessment may have to be reduced if it is greater than the absent parent's **Protected Income**. To calculate the Protected Income,

add:
   i) The Income Support personal allowance for the absent parent, or, if there is a new partner, for that couple;
   ii) The Income Support age-related allowance for each child in the absent parent's household;
   iii) Any relevant Income Support premiums;
   iv) The absent parent's reasonable housing costs (rent or mortgage);

   v) 80% of the absent parent's net Council Tax liability;

  vi) A fixed amount, (£30 in January 1996);

 vii) An allowance for high travel-to-work costs (where appropriate).

This gives the **Basic Protected Income**.

If the total income of the absent parent's household (calculated in the same way as Net Income, but including Child Benefit and called **Disposable Income**) is more than the Basic Protected Income, then 15% of the excess is added to give the **Total Protected Income**.

The effect of this on the assessment is given by the following rules:

—The assessment only 'bites' over the Total Protected Income figure.

—If the Protected Income figure would otherwise stop the assessment 'biting', then a token payment has to be made, with some exceptions. This payment is 10% of the Income Support single adult personal allowance for someone aged 25 or over.

—If the absent parent is on Income Support, then the 10% token amount will still be payable, with some exceptions.

This basic assessment framework is a bit different from the original one. Some new rules have been added, such as:

—Normally no one is expected to pay more than 30% of their net income (though this doesn't apply to absent parents who only pay the minimum amount).

—If you have high travel-to-work costs, an extra allowance might be made.

—If you are an absent parent, and you transferred property and/or capital of at least £5,000 before 5th April 1993 wholly or partly for the benefit of your children, an extra allowance may be made.

More changes are to be made quite soon. These will provide a little discretion by allowing some departures from the formula. However, the possibilities are going to be fairly limited.

They could allow special expenses to be taken into account—such as travel costs not otherwise covered by the regulations (e.g. for contact with the children), particular debts taken on before the separation, expenses arising from a long-term disability, or costs incurred in supporting other children.

They could also allow wider consideration of property or capital transfers.

More scrutiny would be allowed, for example, if a parent's standard of living was much higher than fitted in with stated income, or if housing costs or travel costs seemed unreasonably high.

As you can see the formula doesn't give you a figure at a glance! You really need a lot of fingers and toes (plus a pocket calculator and a steady nerve!) to work out what the amount will be.

In fact, there are quite a lot of other factors which could affect the sums, such as:

—If the mother has children living with her who have different fathers living in different households.

—If the father has children living with him who have different mothers living in different households.

—If the children spend an average of two nights or more per week away from the main carer.

These and various other circumstances will have special rules.

The Agency have a **helpline** and can give you an indication of how much child support maintenance may be payable. Even so, the only certain way to ascertain the amount is to put the matter in the hands of the Child Support Agency.

CSA telephone numbers

☞ p113

The Child Support Agency have very wide powers to obtain information. If the absent parent fails to provide information they may find themselves ordered to pay extra until details are supplied.

If the parent looking after the children is on Income Support, Family Credit, or Disability Working Allowance, and refuses to apply to the Agency for an assessment against the other parent, then a deduction may be made from their Benefit.

To avoid this, you would have to show that you have reasonable grounds for believing there to be a risk of harm or undue distress to you or your child if the Child Support Agency were involved.

On the other hand, if you do not receive Benefit you are not obliged to insist on collecting the sum assessed against the absent partner.

Reasons for Appeal

If you don't agree with a decision made by the Child Support Agency, you can appeal to a Tribunal. Some possible reasons for appeal are:

Appeals

☞ Chapter 21

a) The Calculation of your Income.

You might be able to challenge the calculation of your income—especially if you work varying amounts of overtime or are self-employed.

In an appeal like this you need to supply as clear information as you can about your income.

b) The Risk of Harm or Distress.

You may have refused to co-operate with an assessment because you believe there is a risk of harm or undue distress to you or your child if the Child Support Agency pursues an application.

You would have to explain why you believed there to be a risk. Violence against you or the child during the relationship is one possibility.

For the most part, child support will be fixed by the Agency, though the **courts** will still have to deal with some aspects. Financial support for stepchildren, support for children aged 19 and over, payment of school fees, extra help for disabled children, financial support above the maximum the Child Support Agency can recover, absent parents living outwith the UK— these will have to be sorted out by the courts rather than the Child Support Agency. In addition, the courts will still deal with requests to vary Court Orders made, or arrangements entered into, before April 1993.

For details of financial support for children

☞ Chapter 20

"Hey Dad, it's the CSA"

Because of the phasing-in provisions, the Agency were intending to take on cases where there is an existing arrangement (either a voluntary agreement, a Maintenance Agreement or a Court Order) from April 1996 (unless Income Support, Family Credit or Disability Working Allowance is in payment). However, this date has been put back.

TO THINK ABOUT

You can't rely on being able to opt out of the Agency!

Even if you've informally agreed a figure for child support between you, that won't stop an assessment being calculated **and enforced** by the Child Support Agency if either of you asks them for one. Once the phasing-in period is over, this will be the case even if there is an enforceable formal Agreement.

Remember—if the partner who is due maintenance is receiving Income Support, Family Credit, or Disability Working Allowance, then assessment by the Child Support Agency will almost certainly *have* to be made. It's not your partner's fault!

Another point to note is that in Scotland a child of 12 or over has the right to apply for an assessment, subject to certain conditions.

24

LEGAL AID

Help with legal fees may be available if you are on a low income, and have little or no savings.

Not all legal firms do Legal Aid work. The fees paid to solicitors for this work are lower, and some firms feel that it is time-consuming and uneconomic, taking into account the costs of running an office.

Check that the firm you select does do Legal Aid work. Generally, there is a blue and white logo of two matchstick figures sitting at a table, which will be displayed prominently at the entrance to the solicitor's office, if the firm undertakes Legal Aid work. Otherwise, check on the position when you arrange an appointment.

The best way may be to contact your local Citizens' Advice Bureau, which will have a list of solicitors willing to undertake Legal Aid work.

Two kinds of Legal Aid which apply in tackling family problems are **Advice & Assistance** and **Civil Legal Aid**.

Advice & Assistance

Advice & Assistance covers advice given in a personal interview with a solicitor, or written advice on matters of Scots law on your particular problem.

For example, preliminary advice, which may avoid the need to go to court, can include advising on the terms and the drawing up of a Separation Agreement, and advice on recovering arrears of maintenance payments due to you under a Court Order or written agreement.

Advice & Assistance is available without contribution if you receive Income Support or Family Credit, or have a very low income, and if you have capital under a specified amount. Otherwise, a contribution on a sliding scale will be payable, depending on the amount of income or capital you have.

Your spouse's means would not be taken into account in any matrimonial problem as it would be considered that they have a contrary interest in your dispute. However, if you are living with a new partner, his or her income and savings *are* taken into account in assessing your financial circumstances.

The income and capital limits which determine whether you are eligible, and whether you would have to pay a contribution, are detailed in regulations which are normally updated each year. The Scottish Legal Aid Board publishes a list of these limits each year.

Address
☞ p114

Civil Legal Aid

There is a similar but more detailed financial test of eligibility for Civil Legal Aid. The main difference is that Family Credit is not a passport to Civil Legal Aid without a contribution.

Civil Legal Aid allows you to be represented by a solicitor, or in certain complex circumstances an advocate, in court proceedings such as actions of divorce (except simplified procedure divorces) or other family law matters such as custody, access, interdict, aliment and adoption.

There is a procedure which allows specially urgent work, such as taking preliminary steps in court proceedings or embarking upon a particularly crucial part of these proceedings, to be undertaken by a solicitor without a detailed financial appraisal of your means being completed first by the Legal Aid Board, although you will be asked to provide details at a later stage. Your solicitor will ask for a lot of information before carrying out the work, in order to give you an idea of how you stand.

It is important to note that if a child seeks Legal Aid, that child can be assessed separately—the resources of the parent or person caring for the child are not taken into account.

Money or Property Recovered

If, as a result of legal advice or in a court action, you receive money or property, then the legal fees are recoverable from what you receive.

Monies recovered in an action of aliment or sums by way of periodical allowance—that is, sums payable as maintenance by your spouse—are exempt, as too are certain Benefits and allowances.

Also exempt is the first £2,500 of money or property recovered in divorce proceedings or in any related settlement. Thus if you receive £2,500 you should be able to keep it and have your legal fees paid by the Scottish Legal Aid Board. If you receive £2,750, and your legal fees are say £600, then you should still keep £2,500, but the rest will go towards your legal fees.

If you have received Civil Legal Aid and have paid a contribution towards the costs of the proceedings, that contribution will not normally be refunded by the Scottish Legal Aid Board. Only in exceptional cases, if the cost of the proceedings has been less than the total of your contributions, or the opponent has paid the expenses of the action, are you likely to have your contribution, or part of it, repaid.

If you recover money where you have been advised under Advice & Assistance, the procedure is a little different. In some circumstances, your solicitor can ask that fees should not be deducted from any sum recovered, or property preserved on your behalf, if it would cause you great hardship or would be very difficult to do because of the nature of the property.

Legal Aid and Court Expenses

Usually, if someone loses a court action they have to pay the other person's expenses. However, in family actions there is rarely a clear 'winner' or 'loser'. Often both parties in a family action ask the court for something and both may achieve at least some of what they wanted. In that case it is quite likely that each person would be expected to sort out their own expenses.

If you have Legal Aid, then unless you've been found entitled to more than £2,500 in a divorce action, your own legal fees would be paid out of the Legal Aid fund. If you are found entitled to more than £2,500 in divorce proceedings, any amount in excess of that sum has to be paid to the Legal Aid Board, and that includes any amount in expenses which may be recoverable from the opponent.

This is applied towards the expenses actually incurred by your solicitor, and any shortfall will be met by the fund.

If you recover more than the solicitor's actual or estimated account for fees, the Board will likely agree to pay over most of the excess quickly and account later for any balance which may be due.

There are no hardship provisions in Civil Legal Aid to correspond with those in Advice & Assistance. Even so, if the court decides you *should* pay your partner's expenses, then if you have Civil Legal Aid you can ask the court to modify the actual amount you have to pay. The court will take into account the means of both parties, and their conduct in connection with the proceedings. In some cases the court might decide that nothing has to be paid.

If you are found liable to pay the expenses and your partner has Civil Legal Aid it may be possible for you to negotiate payment by instalments with the Legal Aid Board.

25

POSSIBLE FUTURE DEVELOPMENTS

Family life and family law have both changed a great deal over the last twenty years. Both may change a great deal more over the next twenty.

Grounds for Divorce

Divorce on separation, after one year with consent (instead of two), and two years without consent (instead of five), has been suggested by the Scottish Law Commission.*

One of the reasons for this is so that people would no longer have to use the fault-based grounds for divorce (unreasonable behaviour or adultery) simply to avoid having to wait at least two years for a divorce.

Cohabitation

The Scottish Law Commission have also suggested* that if a couple live together but don't marry, and then separate, some financial claims should be possible, though not such wide claims as those on divorce.

Divorce in England

There are proposals to change divorce procedure in England. These would introduce a year's 'thinking time' after a decision was made to divorce. During this year people would be encouraged to go to counselling if there was any chance for the marriage to be saved. If that wasn't a possibility, then the time would be used to sort out the practical arrangements for the children, property and financial support.

People would be expected to try to use mediation to do this unless there was a good reason not to.

Legal Aid would also be reformed to reflect these changes.

* If you are particularly interested in either supporting or opposing any of these proposals you should talk to your MP about it. You can buy the Scottish Law Commission report containing most of the proposals at HMSO. *Report on Family Law—Scottish Law Commission No. 135.*

26

USEFUL ADDRESSES

Many of the following organisations have centres in various parts of Scotland—phone to check.

Counselling

BROOK ADVISORY CENTRE: **(0131) 229 3596**   (9am - 9pm,
                                                      + ans. m/c)
    2 Lower Gilmore Place, Edinburgh EH3 9NY.

CATHOLIC MARRIAGE ADVISORY COUNCIL:

  –EDINBURGH CENTRE: **(0131) 440 2650**   (10am - 5pm)
    113 Whitehouse Loan, Edinburgh EH9 1BB.

  –GLASGOW CENTRE: **(0141) 204 1239**   (Mon - Thurs,
                                                      10am - 8.30pm)
    196 Clyde Street, Glasgow G1 4JY.

CHURCH OF SCOTLAND BOARD OF SOCIAL RESPONSIBILITY:

  –TOM ALLAN CENTRE: **(0141) 221 1535**   (9am - 5pm)
    23 Elmbank Street, Glasgow G2 4PD.

–Number 21 Counselling Service: **(0131) 221 9377**
(Mon - Thurs 9am - 8pm,
Fri 9am - 5pm)
21 Rutland Square, Edinburgh EH1 2BB.

Edinburgh Health Care—Family Planning and Well
Woman Services: **(0131) 332 7941** (Mon - Thurs 8.30am -
8pm, Fri 8.30am - 4pm,
Sat 9.30am - 12.30pm)
18 Dean Terrace, Edinburgh EH4 1NL.

Glasgow Jewish Counselling Service: **(0141) 422 1472**
(9.30am - 1pm, + ans. m/c)
49 Coplaw Street, Glasgow G41 7JE.

Glasgow Marriage Counselling Service: **(0141) 248 5249**
(10am - 9pm)
Helpline: **(0141) 226 4122** (Mon 6.30 - 8.30pm, Wed
10.30am - 12.30pm, + ans. m/c info)
27 Sandyford Place, Glasgow G3 7NB.

Lothian Marriage Counselling Service: **(0131) 556 1527**
(Mon - Thurs 9am - 9pm,
Fri 9am - 6pm, Sat 9am - 1pm)
9 Dundas Street, Edinburgh EH3 6QG.

Public Counselling Service: **(0141) 950 3359**
Jordanhill Counselling Unit, University of Strathclyde,
76 Southbrae Drive, Jordanhill, Glasgow G13 1PP.

Free counselling service to individuals, by participants on
the Diploma course in Counselling which is run by the
Unit.

THE SCOTTISH COUNCIL ON ALCOHOL: (0141) 333 9677
2nd floor, 166 Buchanan Street, Glasgow G1 2NH.

—provide help for people with alcohol problems.

SOLUTIONS IN THERAPY: (01277) 229992
Swan House, Suite 3, 9 Queens Road,
Brentwood, Essex.

—provide counselling using 'solution-focused brief therapy', which draws on people's strengths and resources in helping with a range of difficulties. There are counsellors in Scotland.

Mediation (child-related)

FAMILY MEDIATION—SCOTLAND: (0131) 220 1610
>   127 Rose Street South Lane, Edinburgh   EH2 4BB.

LOCAL SERVICES:

BORDERS: (01721) 724170
>   Family Mediation Borders,
>   P.O. Box 13753, Peebles   EH45 8ZY.

CENTRAL*: (01786) 472984
>   Family Mediation Central Scotland,
>   16 Melville Terrace, Stirling   FK8 2NE.

DUMFRIES & GALLOWAY: (01387) 263185
>   NCH Action for Children,
>   Dumfries & Galloway FMS,
>   The Family Centre, 4 Cresswell Gardens,
>   Dumfries   DG1 2HH.

FIFE: (01592) 751095
>   NCH Action for Children,
>   Family Mediation Fife,
>   30 North Street, Glenrothes   KY7 5NA.

GRAMPIAN—Family Mediation Grampian:
>   –ABERDEEN: (01224) 630050
>   >   27 Huntly Street, Aberdeen   AB1 1TJ.
>
>   –BANFF & BUCHAN: (01779) 812270
>
>   –MORAY: (01343) 540801
>   >   17 Institution Road, Elgin   IV30 1QT.

HIGHLAND: (01463) 712100
>   Family Mediation Highland,
>   62 Academy Street, Inverness   IV1 1LP.

LOTHIAN*: (0131) 226 4507
Family Mediation Lothian,
37 George Street, Edinburgh EH2 2HN.

ORKNEY: (01856) 870571
Family Mediation Orkney,
43, Junction Road, Kirkwall, Orkney KW15 1AR.

STRATHCLYDE*—Family Mediation Strathclyde:
–GLASGOW: (0141) 332 2731
1 Melrose Street, Glasgow G4 9BJ.

–AYRSHIRE: (01563) 572429
63 Titchfield Street, Kilmarnock KA1 1QS.

TAYSIDE: (01382) 201343
Family Mediation Tayside,
132A Nethergate, Dundee DD1 4ED.

WESTERN ISLES: (01851) 706868
Family Mediation Western Isles,
The Bridge Community Centre, Bayhead,
Stornoway, Isle of Lewis HS1 2DU.

Mediation (child, financial and property matters)

CALM (COMPREHENSIVE ACCREDITED LAWYER MEDIATORS),
CONTACT ANNE MCTAGGART: (01224) 845845
34 Albyn Place, Aberdeen AB9 1FW.

Family lawyers who have had special training in mediation
can be contacted through the above address. Details of
accredited solicitor mediators can also be obtained from
The Law Society of Scotland—see page 114.

* These services also offer mediation on financial and property
matters.

Other Useful Numbers and Addresses

CHILDLINE SCOTLAND: **0800 1111**

24-hour confidential helpline for children with problems.

CHILD SUPPORT AGENCY: **0345 133 133** (national enquiry
line)

The CSA also provide leaflets—phone **0345 830 830**

FAMILY LAW ASSOCIATION,
CONTACT CAROLE SHERIDAN: **(0141) 332 3536**
Sheridan, McDermott & Co.,
166 Buchanan Street, Glasgow G1 2LW.

Lawyers with a particular interest in family law. A list of member solicitors is available from the above address, or from The Law Society—see below.

GINGERBREAD SCOTLAND: **(0141) 353 0953** (10am - 2pm)
Community Centre Halls, 304 Maryhill Road,
Glasgow G20 7YE.

Self-help groups for single parent families.

SCOTTISH ASSOCIATION OF CITIZENS' ADVICE BUREAUX:
(0131) 667 0156
26 George Square, Edinburgh EH8 9LD.

CAB deal with a wide variety of problems, including personal debt and Benefits. There are offices in most towns—see the local telephone book.

THE LAW SOCIETY OF SCOTLAND: (0131) 226 7411
26 Drumsheugh Gardens, Edinburgh EH3 7YR.

—the regulating body for lawyers in Scotland. They deal with enquires from the public, promote legal services and investigate complaints of misconduct against solicitors.

ONE PARENT FAMILIES SCOTLAND: (0131) 556 3899/4563
(9am - 4pm)
13 Gayfield Square, Edinburgh EH1 3NX.

–Also provides an ACCESS CENTRE: **(01382) 501972**
101 Whitfield Drive, Dundee DD4 0DX.

Information, counselling, leaflets and campaigning for single parent families in Scotland.

ONE PLUS—ONE PARENT FAMILIES: (0141) 333 1450
55 Renfrew Street, Glasgow G2 3BD.

Advice, training and campaigning for equal opportunities for single parent families.

SCOTTISH CHILD LAW CENTRE: (0141) 226 3434
ADVICE LINE: (0141) 226 3737
UNDER 18S ONLY: 0800 317 500
4th floor, Cranston House, 108 Argyle Street, Glasgow G2 8BH.

Help with the law relating to young persons.

SCOTTISH LEGAL AID BOARD: (0131) 226 7061
44 Drumsheugh Gardens, Edinburgh EH3 7SW.

SLAB provide a leaflet with information about Legal Aid.

SCOTTISH WOMEN'S AID: (0131) 221 0401 (10am - 1pm,
+ ans. m/c)

12 Torphichen Street, Edinburgh EH3 8JQ.

—the national office of Women's Aid in Scotland, which offers information, support and refuge to abused women and their children (if any). There are 39 local groups throughout Scotland—the numbers are in telephone directories—or call SWA, local police or social work department for nearest contact.

27

PERSONAL & FINANCIAL DETAILS

These pages allow you to gather together and have ready much of the information your solicitor will need.

Fill in the boxes using capitals to make the information easier to read. Put N/A where a heading is Not Applicable or the information Not Available. Note your financial interest at the addresses shown on the Financial Details sheets (Assets and Liabilities).
Give all your names, including 'known as' if different from those shown on your birth certificate.

These pages can be photocopied (and enlarged)—you may find it easier to make copies first and then write on those, so that you needn't worry about making mistakes!

The forms are given in the following order:

i) Personal Details:
  —Your Details
  —Children's Details
  —Partner's Details

ii) Financial Details:
  —Your Income/Expenditure
  —Partner's Income/Expenditure
  —Matrimonial Property (Assets/Liabilities)
  —Non-matrimonial Property.

PERSONAL DETAILS

YOUR DETAILS	
FIRST NAME:	SURNAME:
MIDDLE NAME(S):	MAIDEN AND ANY PREVIOUS MARRIED SURNAMES:
PRESENT ADDRESS:	DATE OF BIRTH:
	TEL. (DAY):
POSTCODE:	

IS THIS ADDRESS THE MATRIMONIAL HOME?   YES/NO

ADDRESS TO BE KEPT CONFIDENTIAL?   YES/NO

PHONE NO. TO BE KEPT CONFIDENTIAL?   YES/NO

CHILDREN'S DETAILS		
FIRST NAME	MIDDLE NAMES	DATE OF BIRTH

PARTNER'S DETAILS	
FIRST NAME:	SURNAME:
MIDDLE NAME(S):	MAIDEN AND ANY PREVIOUS MARRIED SURNAMES:
PRESENT ADDRESS (IF DIFFERENT): POSTCODE:	DATE OF BIRTH: DATE OF MARRIAGE: MARRIAGE REGISTERED AT:
HAS THIS ADDRESS BEEN THE MATRIMONIAL HOME? YES/NO	
PREVIOUS JOINT ADDRESS (IF DIFFERENT): POST CODE:	

FINANCIAL DETAILS

PERIOD FOR WHICH THESE FIGURES APPLY—FROM: [   ]

TO: [   ]

Notes—1. All figures should be for the same period.

—2. Where a figure is not known, give an estimate followed by 'E'.

YOUR OWN INCOME		
SOURCE	NAME AND TEL. NO. OF SOURCE, AND ANY REFERENCE NUMBER	AMOUNT
WORK*		£
INCOME SUPPORT		£
CHILD BENEFIT		£
STATE PENSION		£
PENSION SCHEME		£
BUILDING SOCIETY INTEREST		£
BANK ACCOUNT INTEREST		£
SHARE DIVIDENDS		£
INVESTMENT INTEREST		£
OTHER SOURCES		£
TOTAL INCOME		£

* Take-home pay, including average overtime and bonuses

120

YOUR OWN EXPENDITURE

HOME

RENT	£
LOAN REPAYMENTS (HOUSE)	£
COUNCIL TAX	£
WATER RATES	£
ELECTRICITY	£
GAS	£
COAL	£
TELEPHONE	£
TV RENTAL/LICENCE	£
INSURANCE—BUILDINGS	£
—CONTENTS	£
MAINTENANCE/REPAIRS	£
OTHER:	£

CHILDREN

CLOTHES	£
FOOD (SCHOOL DINNERS)	£
TUITION	£
CHILDCARE	£
HOBBIES/POCKET MONEY	£
SCHOOL OUTINGS	£
OTHER:	£

LIVING

FOOD	£
MILK	£
CLOTHES	£
SHOES	£
MEDICATION/DENTIST	£
NEWSPAPERS/MAGAZINES	£
ENTERTAINMENT	£
MEALS OUT	£
HOLIDAYS/TRIPS	£
OTHER:	£

HOLIDAY HOME PAYMENTS	£
BANK LOAN/OVERDRAFT	£
CREDIT CARD INTEREST	£
PENSION SCHEME	£
LIFE ASSURANCE	£

TRANSPORT

CAR—FUEL	£
—LOAN REPAYMENTS	£
—INSURANCE	£
—ROAD TAX	£
—SERVICING	£
BUS FARES	£
TRAIN FARES	£
TAXI FARES	£

TOTAL EXPENDITURE	£

PARTNER'S INCOME		
SOURCE	NAME AND TEL. NO. OF SOURCE, AND ANY REFERENCE NUMBER	AMOUNT
WORK*		£
INCOME SUPPORT		£
CHILD BENEFIT		£
STATE PENSION		£
PENSION SCHEME		£
BUILDING SOCIETY INTEREST		£
BANK ACCOUNT INTEREST		£
SHARE HOLDINGS DIVIDENDS		£
INVESTMENT INTEREST		£
OTHER SOURCES		£
TOTAL INCOME		£

* Take-home pay, including average overtime and bonuses

PARTNER'S EXPENDITURE

HOME

RENT	£
LOAN REPAYMENTS (HOUSE)	£
COUNCIL TAX	£
WATER RATES	£
ELECTRICITY	£
GAS	£
COAL	£
TELEPHONE	£
TV RENTAL/LICENCE	£
INSURANCE—BUILDINGS	£
—CONTENTS	£
MAINTENANCE/REPAIRS	£
OTHER:	£

CHILDREN

CLOTHES	£
FOOD (SCHOOL DINNERS)	£
TUITION	£
CHILDCARE	£
HOBBIES/POCKET MONEY	£
SCHOOL OUTINGS	£
OTHER:	£

LIVING

FOOD	£
MILK	£
CLOTHES	£
SHOES	£
MEDICATION/DENTIST	£
NEWSPAPERS/MAGAZINES	£
ENTERTAINMENT	£
MEALS OUT	£
HOLIDAYS/TRIPS	£
OTHER:	£

HOLIDAY HOME PAYMENTS	£
BANK LOAN/OVERDRAFT	£
CREDIT CARD INTEREST	£
PENSION SCHEME	£
LIFE ASSURANCE	£

TRANSPORT

CAR—FUEL	£
—LOAN REPAYMENTS	£
—INSURANCE	£
—ROAD TAX	£
—SERVICING	£
BUS FARES	£
TRAIN FARES	£
TAXI FARES	£

TOTAL EXPENDITURE	£

MATRIMONIAL PROPERTY

DATE ON WHICH THESE FIGURES APPLY: [   ]

Note—All valuations and estimates should be for the date of separation,
or today's date if you are not separated.

MATRIMONIAL ASSETS	OWN £	PARTNER'S £	JOINT £
MATRIMONIAL HOME			
HOLIDAY HOME/TIMESHARE			
BANK ACCOUNT			
BUILDING SOCIETY			
SHARE HOLDINGS			
HOUSEHOLD CONTENTS			
VEHICLES			
PENSION FUNDS (use transfer value as a guide)			
INSURANCE POLICIES (use surrender value as a guide)			
OTHER:			
TOTAL ASSETS	£	£	£

MATRIMONIAL LIABILITIES	OWN £	PARTNER'S £	JOINT £
HOME LOAN (MORTGAGE)			
CAR LOAN			
BANK LOAN			
CREDIT CARD			
OTHER:			
TOTAL LIABILITIES	£	£	£

TOTALS		
TOTAL MATRIMONIAL ASSETS:	£	
TOTAL MATRIMONIAL LIABILITIES:	— £	
NET MATRIMONIAL PROPERTY:	= £	

NON-MATRIMONIAL PROPERTY (ACQUIRED BEFORE MARRIAGE— E.G. LEGACIES, PERSONAL GIFTS, REDUNDANCY PAYMENTS, ETC.)	OWN £	PARTNER'S £	JOINT £
TOTAL NON-MATRIMONIAL PROPERTY	£	£	£

Name	Tel.	Address	Appointment Date/Time

INDEX

This section provides a quick and easy way of finding some of the terms you will come across when discussing separation and divorce. The list is not exhaustive—use the Table of Contents for locating general topics.